BWB Texts

Short books on big subjects from great New Zealand writers

Time of Useful Consciousness

Acting Urgently on Climate Change

RALPH CHAPMAN

Published in 2015 by Bridget Williams Books Limited, PO Box 12474,
Wellington 6144, New Zealand, www.bwb.co.nz, info@bwb.co.nz.

ISBN 9780908321414 (Paperback), ISBN 9780908321421 (EPUB)
ISBN 9780908321438 (KINDLE), ISBN 9780908321445 (PDF)
ISTC A02201500000012D
DOI 10.7810/9780908321414

A catalogue record for this book is available from the National Library
of New Zealand. Kei te pātenga raraunga o Te Puna Mātauranga o
Aotearoa te whakarārangi o tēnei pukapuka

Acknowledgements
The publisher acknowledges the ongoing support provided by the
Bridget Williams Books Publishing Trust and Creative New Zealand.

An earlier version of this text was presented in November 2012 as an
invited lecture to the University of Auckland, the annual Chapman
Lecture in honour of Professor Robert Chapman, who was founding
Professor of Political Studies at the university.

Publisher: Tom Rennie
Cover and internal design: Base Two
Editors: Geoff Walker and Ginny Sullivan
Typesetter: Tina Delceg
Printer: Printlink, Wellington

CONTENTS

INTRODUCTION

I have worked on climate change policy since 1988, the year in which Jim Hansen, a famous US climate scientist, first testified before Congress about climate change, and in which the Intergovernmental Panel on Climate Change was established. Every year over this quarter of a century, I have looked for signs of real change, indications that the global community was getting to grips with the climate change issue. Every year I also looked for signs of policy progress in New Zealand, and occasionally I saw some. But progress has been frustratingly slow. Almost every year global carbon emissions have risen, and through most of this period New Zealand's emissions have continued to rise as well. Looking back over this quarter-century, the picture is a disturbing one. The rate at which the public has been growing more conscious about climate change, and at which politicians have taken tangible policy action, is dismally slow.

Why, then, do I continue to have hope for substantive action?

We know that human institutions are slow to change. With something as embedded as the burning of fossil fuels for around 80 per cent of global energy, we can expect enormous inertia. We also know that it is a basic human tendency to delay action on a growing problem – when such action requires discomfort and disruption – until the last minute. Such 'just-in-time' responses may work with small and manageable problems, but if such an approach is taken to complex legacy problems such as climate change, the results are likely to be disastrous.[1] I have seen this at close quarters in international climate change negotiations. I have also seen, at first hand, the intense lobbying efforts of special interests to slow down action on climate change. The unsurprising tendency of politicians is to succumb to this pressure, despite knowing how the likely negative effects of delay will impact on the lives of children already born, as well as future generations.

These realities and these delays mean that we cannot know whether the global community will act in time to prevent climate change becoming an ungovernable problem. Nobel Prize-winning economist Paul Krugman has compared our situation to a gamble with civilisation, in which

we have, without knowing it, made an immensely dangerous bet that we'll be able to use the power and knowledge we've gained in the past couple of centuries to cope with the climate risks we've unleashed over the same period.[2]

At the same time, it strikes me as vital to stay optimistic – to build the impetus to limit climate change as much as possible by taking tangible individual actions and adopting innovative public policies. Another compelling reason not to give up is the moral argument that we should do the right thing by those – typically with the least resources – who will feel the impacts of climate change first or most severely.

Data released in early 2015 by the International Energy Agency (IEA), estimating that global carbon emissions did not rise in 2014, are very encouraging. So was the US–China agreement of November 2014 when Presidents Xi Jinping of China and Barack Obama of the United States agreed on a pact in which China's emissions would start falling by 2030 at the latest, and US emissions would be reduced faster than previously over the next decade, namely by 27 per cent by 2025 relative to 2005 levels. This was immensely good news for the global community – at last the two biggest emitters had agreed on concrete goals that put these two economies on a positive path. This could even inspire a wider, credible climate agreement in Paris at the end of 2015. However, there are several big 'ifs and buts' to be considered.

First, the message that the global community on the whole wants rapid action to reduce climate threats has not yet been heard by some international leaders, such as Stephen Harper of Canada, Tony Abbott of Australia and, arguably, Vladimir Putin of Russia. The American political system – despite Mr Obama's important forward steps under the Clean Air Act – may become hamstrung by a Republican majority in both houses of Congress opposed to substantive climate action. Furthermore, there is no assurance after 2016 that a future US president will be disposed to stick to a decade-long agreement with China.

Second, the US–China agreement is not enough in itself to hold global warming below the important warming guardrail of 2°C. This might not matter if 2°C was only a number, but it is symbolic of cumulative human impact and in fact represents a significant scientific milestone on the road between dangerous and catastrophic warming.[3] Warming of 2°C will bring with it major climate changes, perhaps enough in themselves to really stretch human coping abilities. While the IEA's recent data about global emissions are encouraging, until net emissions fall to near zero globally, concentrations of greenhouse gases in the atmosphere (the stock of emissions remaining in the atmosphere) will continue to rise. It is these rising concentrations that really drive rising temperatures and other aspects of climate change.

But even if global emissions do not continue rising, or start falling gradually from now on, they are unlikely to fall fast enough to avoid pushing global warming past 2°C. So there is still a critical race to be run between the mounting concentrations of greenhouse gases in the atmosphere, which could take global average temperature up by 3 or even 4°C, and policy action designed to cut these concentrations and avoid the worst consequences.

What will be the outcome of this race? It's a huge question for all countries, including New Zealand. Reframing it, can we win the race between greening the economy to reduce emissions, and the rising wave of damage and dislocation caused by climate change? And how can we best make use of the shrinking window of time – maybe only a decade or two – before our society has to confront very diminished and uncomfortable choices, and risks starting to lose its ability to take coherent action in the face of the pressures from climate destabilisation? There are many calls on this small space of time, but nevertheless it gives us an opportunity to take action to green our economy and cut emissions, while preserving a future with a high quality of life, as the multiple impacts from climate change grow more relentless, and the stresses on our social and political institutions intensify.

Taking advantage of this window depends on us anticipating the impacts of climate damage, actively reassessing our goals, and getting under way a rapid energy transformation before our democratic institutions, society and economy come under such stress that they start to function poorly. Fortunately, despite patchy central government policy action to date in New Zealand, there are hopeful signs of rising awareness both in New Zealand and abroad. There is also an emerging take-up of key technologies and behaviours that could build into a credible transition to a markedly greener and lower-carbon economy and society.

I start with a brief look at the urgency of climate change mitigation, an assessment based largely on the physical science. This aspect is arguably the less contentious part of a complex picture. There are fewer value judgements involved – it is a more objective domain, especially in terms of its main findings.[4] But it is remarkable how much heat even this physical science debate generates, not – in general – among scientists[5] but among those interpreting the science and drawing inferences about implied policy change.[6] Disinformation has added much of the heat.[7]

Then, turning to policy, I ask what forces are acting *against* solving this challenge of taking sufficient policy action to hold and then cut emissions – and cutting those emissions *fast* enough and far enough to avoid highly damaging global change. I evaluate the firmly held view of most economists that a price on carbon will drive decarbonisation most effectively. Is this misleading? Also, when the case for change is urgent, how should we think about a bottom-up or top-down negotiated approach? And I reconsider the widespread assumption that the solution is all about technology.

More rapid action to cut emissions, I suggest, depends heavily on the breadth of support for inter-related energy, transport, urban and other solutions; and on a commitment to integrated policy aimed at accelerating green economic and social transformation. This transformation needs to go beyond an incremental transition. It will not occur in New Zealand without a sense of urgency and a coherent framing of the issues, including a positive vision of a green economy. That vision looks rather like today's world, but with a range of technologies and social practices that are demonstrably greener. I outline later some crucial aspects of the vision, relating to energy, transport and cities. The vision also needs to extend to agriculture and forestry, which have an important role to play, but which I cannot cover in this essay.

Overshadowing all these elements is the need to act fast to maintain our democratic institutions, given the pressures of intensifying climate change and the potential for poor policy decisions under increasing time pressure. We need to be alive to the risks to good policy-making and to democratic processes that are created by the pressure on governments under a rapidly tightening time constraint. We can see the window I have referred to as a 'time of useful consciousness', using the aeronautical term meaning 'the time between when one loses oxygen, and when one passes out, the brief time in which some life-saving action is possible'.[8] What actions in this time period are truly vital?

1. RUNNING OUT OF TIME

The increasingly numerous and intensely destructive storms and other 'weather events', as the media tend to call them, are a taste of climate change to come. The scientists are clear that a more energetic and humid atmosphere, higher sea surface temperatures and higher ocean levels in a warmer world will in future raise the occurrences of such destructive weather events and the size of their impacts.[1]

From the ranks of the scientists, and many reputable international organisations, the chorus about climate change has become more and more emphatic. The ice and snow scientists of the International Cryosphere Climate Initiative, for example, say 'The cryosphere is on an accelerated warming path … The window for action is closing fast.' Echoing this in a well-worn metaphor, the

World Bank states: 'The science [of climate change] is settled … Our world is on thin ice.'[2]

In 2013 the Intergovernmental Panel on Climate Change (IPCC) – an unprecedented voluntary collaborative effort of scientists around the world – unveiled the first part of its fifth assessment report, focusing on the physical science evidence of climate change. The report confirmed the emerging patterns of climatic change, increasingly evident over the period since the IPCC started reporting almost a generation ago, in 1990. For example, it stated that the average rate of Greenland ice sheet loss has very likely substantially increased from 34 billion tonnes per year in the 1990s to over 200 billion tonnes per year since 2002.[3]

The insurance industry keeps its own collations of climate change impacts, as it is uniquely exposed in a financial sense to the intensification of climate change. Munich Re, the world's largest reinsurer, collates the number of meteorological, hydrological and climatological 'loss' events. Like the IPCC pooling science data, reinsurance company data represent the pooling of huge amounts of diverse insurance claim information. Their figures show a menacing upward trend in the number of events.[4] If it were just the dollar loss value of events, sceptics might be more inclined to dismiss the trend, since the upward trend might be explained simply by a rise in the value of the properties exposed. But it is difficult to wave away an upward curve in carefully counted event *numbers*.

Such trends force us to ask: how rapidly are we running out of time under a 'business as usual' trajectory; and, conversely, how long do we have to make emission reductions that have a good chance of avoiding major climate instability? This is not only a physical science question about the speed and momentum in the climate change trajectory; it is also an economic, social and political question, around the extent of climate disruption that is socially and politically acceptable, and who will be most affected.

PHYSICAL TIPPING POINTS

The interaction of physical and economic aspects has been addressed by a range of models (with varying parameters) representing the climate-economy system, such as the aptly named 'DICE' (dynamic integrated climate economy) model and many others.[5] Such modelling is worth a closer look. The modellers generally indicate that the time left to 'take' total global emissions over a peak and drastically cut emissions in such a way as to stabilise the climate without excessive warming or other disruption, and stay within the 2°C warming guardrail, now appears very short.[6] For example, some modellers suggest five to ten years to start coming down from that peak, and less time if the global rate of emission reduction is slow after the peak.[7] On the optimistic side, some modelling suggests that if the global rate of emission reduction is a more stringent 3 to 5 per cent per year from now, we may *just* stay within the 2°C guardrail.[8] Others debate this, arguing that 'any contextual interpretation of the science demonstrates that the threshold of 2°C is no longer viable, at least within orthodox political and economic constraints'.[9] Another way of saying this is that climate change mitigation commitments (to 2°C) are probably incompatible with continuing shorter-term economic growth, unless that growth is very heavily focused on measures such as renewable energy development targeted at reducing emissions.

To be more specific about some of these risks, consider the debate about physical tipping points – points of no return. The world's two major ice sheets may in both cases be very close to tipping point and, because they are huge, they matter. The Greenland ice sheet may pass an irreversible melting threshold at *around 1.6°C* above pre-industrial temperatures (that is, about 0.7°C from today's temperatures), according to a recent 'best estimate' of the tipping point.[10] That is, we are very likely to pass this tipping point on our current track. This ice sheet's melting could, over a number of centuries, raise the oceans an average of around

6 metres, although some recent science suggests it might stop at around 1 metre.

But adding to Greenland's impact are major risks to sea-level rise from melting of the West Antarctic and East Antarctic ice sheets, as reported in two recent and significant papers.[11] The net result could be more like 15 metres of sea-level rise, over perhaps twenty centuries, a shorter period than that over which some cities, such as London, have existed.[12] Along with this, ice and snow scientists state that 'much of the cryosphere is under threat in at most decades, rather than centuries'.[13] That means less snowpack and meltwater to keep people alive, and to keep agriculture and other industries going.

Another tipping point could be in the ocean's overturning circulation – which drives the Gulf Stream warming the UK and Scandinavia, and affects the deep oceans – according to New Zealand scientist Ron Prinn, who leads a modelling group at MIT.[14] Prinn estimates that around 2.7°C of warming could be a critical tipping point in regard to circulation.

Given the difficulty of changing sufficiently our social and economic patterns of production and consumption, discussed more below, it is very likely just a matter of time before we pass the first of these likely tipping points, 1.6°C. But tipping points beyond 2°C are further away, perhaps in the latter part of the century. Could such tipping points be avoided?

Perhaps. Current unconditional emission reduction pledges are estimated to put us on a trajectory of around 3°C by 2100. But the recent action record of countries is estimated to lead to about 3.9°C, as the actual performance record is somewhat more disappointing than the pledges.[15] Unless decisive action is firmly pledged in the Durban–Paris negotiating process, scheduled to culminate in December 2015, it seems unlikely that the international community will do significantly better than a path that takes us to around 3°C by 2100. Such a dangerous outcome can still be averted, but time is short. Given the risks such as Prinn's oceanic tipping point, it will be necessary for countries to strengthen their 'ambition', to use a term from the negotiations.

Tipping points are one thing, but the insidious rise of temperatures and associated myriad changes in all aspects of the global climate system may also pose large threats in the next few decades. For many people, as temperatures rise there is an escalating threat of extreme heat impacts, as projected by scientists.

Modelling suggests that two broad warming scenarios confront us. One scenario is associated with rapid mitigation, limiting the increase in extreme heat wave exposure on land to a severalfold increase by 2040. There was an example of extreme heat in 2003 in Europe when around 30,000 people died. The other scenario is a 'business as usual' (slow-action) scenario. This is estimated to result in extreme heat events occurring in about 85 per cent of global land area by 2100, with attendant heat-related deaths, massive forest fires and harvest losses. Either of these scenarios is shocking, the latter particularly so.[16]

SOCIAL AND POLITICAL TIPPING POINTS

Earlier I mentioned that urgency is not just a physical science question but also a social and political issue. It is clear that delay in taking action means more climate destabilisation, and more impacts. Many of these are currently unknown by those people and groups on whom the impact will fall. Their interests are not being adequately taken into account by those who understand – at least in the abstract – what is likely to happen as a consequence of global trends, but who turn away from considering the impacts. The estimated 50,000 Russians who died in the 2010 heatwave and fires might have taken a different view on acceptable risk than policy-makers protected from disruption in other parts of the world.[17]

Everyone knows intuitively that delay means greater risk. But the nature of that risk and the rapidity with which delay is adding to risk is not widely understood. As the chair of the US Council on Foreign Relations and a former Treasury Secretary, Robert Rubin, put it recently, this risk is becoming a systemic one for the US economy, and necessitates a protective response:

We do not face a choice between protecting our environment or protecting our economy. We face a choice between protecting our economy by protecting our environment — or allowing environmental havoc to create economic havoc.[18]

The warnings about delay have been sounding for some time now. McKinsey and Company stated in 2009 that 'a delay of 10 years, with action starting in 2020 instead of 2010, would … make it challenging to limit global warming to the 3 degree Celsius threshold …'.[19]

More recently, the IEA has emphasised that delay also rapidly raises the *costs* of cutting emissions. Consider the phenomenon of capital 'lock-in'. Capital investment has a long lifetime if it is not to be written off. Year by year, the current global economic trajectory locks in more and more emissions-generating capital, such as fossil-fuel-fired power stations, and motorways, which investors will understandably be reluctant to see stranded. Conversely, early action can increase the potential for accelerated learning and reduced costs.[20]

Japan has now turned away from nuclear power in the wake of Fukushima and is building coal- and gas-fired power stations.[21] Australia has been constructing new coal-mining and exporting facilities. New Zealand has been promoting deep-sea hydrocarbon exploration. And a number of other countries' actions are not at all consistent with staying inside the 2°C guardrail. If the world community were serious about its 2009 commitment at Copenhagen to stay inside the guardrail, it would be acting very differently and every year's delay in acting to cut emissions would be acknowledged as extremely costly.[22] The IEA report just cited states (*my emphasis added*):

If internationally co-ordinated action is not implemented by 2017, we project that all permissible CO_2 emissions in the 450 Scenario [a scenario that gives a roughly even chance of staying below ~2°C warming] will come from the infrastructure [such as power stations] then existing, so that all new infrastructure from then [2017] until 2035 would need to be *zero-carbon*. This would theoretically be possible at very high cost, but probably not practicable in political terms.

In the US, the White House has come to a similar conclusion: delay in cutting emissions is so costly that delay cannot be justified.[23] It estimates that 'the cost of hitting a specific climate target increases, on average, by approximately 40 percent for each decade of delay'. As we come closer to the 2°C threshold, those costs will rise faster.

What these points together make clear is that although we as a world community are dicing with huge risks, we are showing little grasp of the meaning of urgency. We are not seeing in a clear way the implications of how urgent climate change has become. So, is uncertainty the obstacle?

Much has been written – including by insightful observers such as Naomi Oreskes – about how uncertainty has been manipulated to raise doubts about acting on climate change. But using uncertainty as a basis for delay is a pernicious inversion of logic. Rather, uncertainty suggests we should be more cautious. As Jim Hansen has noted, his far-sighted 1988 prognostication of global warming was 'too optimistic'.[24] Nicholas Stern has made similar comments, stating in 2013 that, had he known the way the situation would change, 'I think I would have been a bit more blunt. I would have been much more strong about the risks of a four- or five-degree [global temperature] rise.'[25] Given the stakes, and the uncertainty with a very negative downside, there is a strong case for immediate precautionary action to cut emissions very steeply.[26] So the next question is, how might this be done?

2. THE NATURE OF OUR RESPONSE

RESPONDING TO THE SCIENCE: HOW SOON?

In shaping a response to this rapidly growing threat, we first need to ask how rapidly we need to cut emissions. In answering this, let us start from the global picture.

The rate of emissions reductions now required, after years of delay in recognising the mounting climate change problem, presents a huge challenge for the world economy, even for developed countries with ample resources. Modellers from the UK's Tyndall Centre, Kevin Anderson and Alice Bows, estimate that the rate of reduction of emissions needed for a reasonable chance of holding global warming to 2°C is more than 5 per cent per year, and this may be just too challenging for developed country democratic systems to cope with.[1] Of course, we could take a huge risk and push this trajectory out a few decades, but that would significantly amplify the risks of exceeding 2°C and be ethically indefensible.

Another way of approaching this question is to ask: will the world be able to cut emissions to near zero (net) by around 2050 or 2060, that is, about a generation from now? A useful thought experiment for those over forty years old is to think back thirty-five years to 1980, and consider the seemingly short period since then. Is such a period long enough, looking forward, to enable a complete transformation of the global energy system? In the past, transformational and rapid change has occurred in some sectors, such as computing and telecommunications, but there has not been such a huge change in the energy system without economic collapse or instability, such as came about with the collapse of the Soviet Union, or when societies are at war.

However, changes in emissions in the past are not a definitive guide to what can be achieved, as they were not made under conditions of *deliberate* policy change. The question is: guided by high carbon prices, but also using a range of strong complementary policy tools, can transformative changes be made? Can changes to renewable energy, and other policies for emission cuts in transport, housing, industry and other areas of energy use, go fast enough to add up to, say, 5 per cent carbon cuts per year? Some argue that the technology is there or emerging.[2] But in New Zealand and most other nations, the supporting policy measures, including the supporting behavioural incentives, have not yet been rolled out. The experimentation has not been attempted. In short, we just do not know until we really try it.

A big barrier is likely to be political will: the democratic governance hurdle. The history of climate policy internationally and domestically is one in which special interests have so far often prevailed.[3] We can reasonably question whether it is in the interests of powerful elites, who wield the most influence in our democracies, to now set aside their own special interests to solve the global climate problem fast enough. For transformative change, intense public pressure on decision-makers will be needed to overcome special-interest lobbying and allow the emergence of truly creative solutions.

Capitalism – the adaptable beast that Anatole Kaletsky describes in his book *Capitalism 4.0*[4] – is not only damaging when unguided but is also highly responsive if the conditions are right. *If and when* it is guided by sufficiently strong democratic pressure and policy, such as in the Scandinavian countries, the Netherlands and Germany, and forced to deal with its own shortcomings, it can undoubtedly respond remarkably quickly and positively. Under these conditions, the necessary rates of emission reduction, around 5 per cent per year, might just be achieved.

However, as I will discuss later, in the liberal market economies, where power and wealth are increasingly concentrated in a small elite, such rapid adjustment seems unlikely because of the current distaste for strong government guidance or regulation. New Zealand has tended to adopt rather purist neoliberal 'self-denying' policies over the last generation, with the international spread of neoliberal orthodoxy, despite the efforts of the 1999–2008 Helen Clark years to emphasise sustainability.[5] In New Zealand, as elsewhere, there has been a powerful nexus among those who own capital but have not been able to envisage a credible adjustment path toward a greener economy. To date, John Key's government has given only lukewarm support to the green economy idea. The business organisation Pure Advantage, for example, has seen its efforts to promote green growth treated sceptically by the government.[6] Phillip Mills, a founder of Pure Advantage, has commented that National's hesitation 'shows the serious gaps in [its] long-term economic strategy'.[7]

At the same time, there has been an increasingly strong line of argument from the Organisation for Economic Co-operation and Development (OECD), the World Bank, the IEA and others that a low-carbon, green economy is an attainable and necessary goal.[8] The World Bank, fearful about the enormous impact of 4°C warming, makes a strong plea for 'turning down the heat' through a range of rapid mitigation measures.[9]

One international climate change authority, Bert Metz, for example, notes that while the Kyoto Protocol succeeded in driving down Kyoto Protocol country emissions by 20 per cent overall by 2010, compared with 1990 levels, the global governance model embodied in the Protocol now needs updating to a different process.[10] He argues that wide take-up of green economy ideas and measures would create a global dynamic that could collectively deal with climate change.

What would this mean for New Zealand? The Danish and Swedish strategies probably give the best answer. These strategies are backed by detailed planning for transforming their economies stage by stage to zero carbon – in Denmark's case by 2050.[11] It is neither cost-free nor impossibly costly. An estimate of the cost of the Danish plan is 1 Euro per day per household, over a forty-year period.

A PRICE ON CARBON: NECESSARY, BUT NOT ENOUGH

Climate policy, or the matter of what to do, has tended to focus on putting a price on carbon. But all the delays and equivocation, both in New

Zealand and in other countries, now mean it looks very unlikely that a price on carbon alone will be sufficient to avert highly dangerous levels of climate change.

Among most economists, price is by far the preferred incentive mechanism for changing behaviour, but a purist focus on price can come at the expense of creative thinking about other policy approaches and instruments whose application may be more complex, but also more politically palatable. Beyond economists, one finds that scientific experts are not always convinced about the centrality of price signals. For example, the IPCC's working group looking at how to reduce carbon emissions in the building sector concluded in 2014 that '[e]xperience shows that pricing is less effective than programmes and regulation (medium evidence, medium agreement)'.[12]

The centrality of prices has long been evident within the New Zealand government, for example, in Treasury advice, where the primacy of the emissions trading scheme (ETS) appears to be an article of faith.[13] This is curious given the evidence that since the ETS came into effect in 2009 it has had remarkably little impact. The core problem is that even if a carbon price is a powerful instrument in principle, political sentiment in New Zealand, as in many countries, is unlikely to allow the implementation of a price that is sufficiently high to make a major difference any time soon.

Conventional economists tend to think about 'optimising' climate change, by aiming for the level of emissions that neatly equates ('at the margin') the *abatement* cost of carbon with the *damage* cost of carbon. The marginal abatement cost is the cost of cutting emissions by an additional 1 tonne. The damage cost is the benefit from damage avoided by 1 tonne less of emissions.

Let us leave aside for the moment questions about whether it is practical to calculate accurately these 'cost curves' or whether such an equation builds a sufficient framework when it ignores ethics. Let us simply consider the conclusions that have been emerging from a great deal of recent work using this framework as the basis of policy advice on climate change.

Some economists suggest the damage cost at this magic margin, referred to as the (optimal) social cost of carbon, could be around US$100 to $400 per tonne of carbon dioxide (CO_2). The answer depends on a range of factors, including 'discount rates', which reflect how we value the lives of future generations, and the shape of the damage cost curve, or how we think damages will increase with emissions and global temperatures.[14] Other economists, such as Yale University's William Nordhaus, have calculated lower numbers for the social cost of carbon, although their estimates have increased over time.[15]

Not surprisingly, some of Nordhaus's assumptions have been challenged even by economists of a similar ilk, notably Nicholas Stern. The essence of their challenge is that when climate damage is more realistically incorporated into climate models, Nordhaus's conclusions on the social cost of carbon and the optimal speed of abatement are demonstrably too low. Stern and colleagues suggest the social cost numbers should be up to NZ\$128 per tonne of CO_2, rising within two decades to more than twice these levels.

If discount rates, an important input into these calculations, are not to discriminate by year of birth, and if the impact of climate change on economic growth is taken into account,[16] then optimal social cost estimates would be higher still. And, more recently, other economists have confirmed that when more care is taken to estimate climate impacts on growth, the social cost of carbon figures should be higher.[17] Taken together, this neoclassical economic literature, for all its limitations, points to a need for a carbon price of at least around NZ\$100 per tonne, markedly higher than the price of under \$7 at which carbon units have recently been trading in New Zealand.

In New Zealand many have concerns at the downturn in international carbon prices, a fall accentuated by factors such as the depreciation of 'certified emission reduction' units, that is, units created under the Kyoto Protocol's 'Clean Development Mechanism' (CDM). The CDM was designed to allow developing nations to make emissions reductions that could then be sold to developed countries, such as the US and New Zealand. In New Zealand's case, emitters have also been able to buy, with few restrictions until May 2015, international carbon units under the rules of New Zealand's ETS; the abundant supply of these units has pushed down the local unit price.[18] The application of the ETS itself has been narrowed by the current government. The entry of agricultural gases into the scheme was delayed indefinitely, and a 'two for one' discount, whereby emitters in the stationary energy, transport and industrial process sectors must only surrender 1 unit for every 2 tonnes of CO_2 they emit, was extended. Considering that agricultural gases (methane and nitrous oxide) account for a substantial part of New Zealand's greenhouse gases, the exclusion of these gases is problematic – it acts to impose a higher burden on the rest of the economy.

The weakness of New Zealand's ETS in delivering an effective price on carbon has been noticed abroad. The reputational damage to New Zealand has been compounded by the decision of the government to walk away from the second

Figure 1 New Zealand's gross and net historical emissions, targets, and gross and net projected emissions under current settings

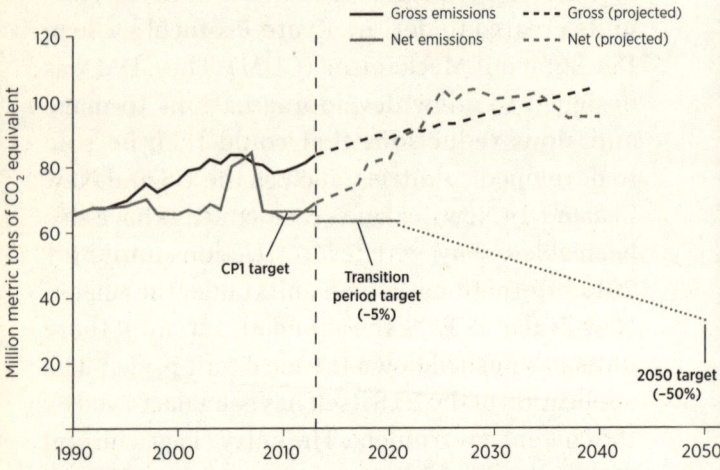

Note: Net emissions are projected to rise rapidly post-2012 due to forest harvesting. In granting permission to reproduce this graph the Ministry for the Environment supplied a list of caveats and requested they be included in this publication – the list can be found in the Notes section.[19]

Source: MfE, 'Environmental Stewardship for a Prosperous New Zealand: Briefing for Incoming Ministers 2014', Wellington, 2014, p.22, www.mfe.govt.nz/sites/default/files/media/About/environment-bim-final.pdf (accessed 8 July 2015).

commitment period under the legally binding Kyoto Protocol, and instead elect to make a 2020 target commitment under the 'best endeavours' Framework Convention. This put at risk New Zealand's hard-earned reputation in climate policy, built up by ministers such as Simon Upton and David Parker, and meant that New Zealand was no longer eligible to buy cheap emission-reduction units on the international market, an own goal for the government.[20]

The warning bells have been ringing for years about the ineffectiveness of any carbon-trading system if carbon prices remain low.[21] The Ministry for the Environment (MfE) projected in 2009 that even at a significantly higher projected price than the minimal price that currently prevails, New Zealand's emissions would be little reduced.[22] The government also estimated in 2011 that even a relatively high carbon price ($100 per tonne) scenario would only cut energy emissions by about 7 per cent below business as usual by 2030.[23]

Recently, MfE's 2014 'Briefing for Incoming Ministers' made starkly clear the large gap between current projections of greenhouse gas emissions and New Zealand's 2050 target of a 50 per cent cut.[24] Figure 1 shows that gross emissions are projected to trend *upwards*, to well above the 2050 target; New Zealand is clearly nowhere near meeting the government's own target using the currently configured ETS and associated policy measures. Moreover, the figure shows a rapidly rising projection for 'net emissions', driven by forest harvesting. It is expected that the government will try to close the yawning gap by applying accounting rules that carry over surplus units from the first or second Kyoto commitment periods, without making a serious attempt to cut gross emissions.

Even more recently, the government announced its climate target for 2030, and this implies an even less ambitious pathway than its weak 2050 target. Indeed, its interim 2030 target has been widely criticised at home and abroad as inadequate and inconsistent with staying within the 2°C guardrail. Expert European analysts Climate Action Tracker noted that if most other countries were to follow New Zealand's approach, global warming would exceed 3–4°C.[25] Moreover, no policies have yet been announced that would get New Zealand to either its 2030 or 2050 targets, so these targets remain empty promises.

If New Zealand were to treat seriously the precautionary principle (which we as a country put our name to at the time of the Rio Convention in 1992) and adopt an insurance framework, taking into account the risks of nasty climate surprises and future stranded assets, the price of carbon would need to be lifted initially to something around $100 per tonne and placed on a rising trajectory.[26] Under current policy, emissions are officially projected by 2020 to be a daunting 29 per cent above the 1990 level (130 per cent if one takes into account the forestry sector).[27] In the face of such an emissions trajectory, a low price on carbon, as the current ETS entails, is ludicrous. It is conceivable that the government might be investing in credible mitigation efforts overseas (that is, earning carbon credits by investing to cut emissions elsewhere) under a 'global responsibility' approach, while doing little mitigation domestically, but there is no sign of this. Only a substantial and rising price on carbon accompanied by strong other measures – discussed later – would enable New Zealand to start transforming its economy in the way that is now needed. It would also reduce the fiscal risk associated with the current apparent plan of buying carbon credits offshore in future years in the event that New Zealand's pleas for advantageous accounting rules fall on deaf ears.

To give an example, an ETS price of say NZ$100 per tonne would have the effect of lifting petrol prices around 20c per litre, which would be less than a sixth of early 2015 pump prices.[28] At around 6 per cent of this recently, the ETS price level amounts to tokenism, or what the Parliamentary Commissioner for the Environment called 'almost toothless'.[29]

A more general concern about reliance on an ETS relates to institutional inertia – New Zealand's ETS involves extended allocations to emitters of free units, commitments that, once made, are difficult to withdraw or amend. Prices can also not be pushed up overnight. Some British and US experts state:

The time required to create [carbon markets], manage them and deal with the problems they inevitably raise …

has meant that 10 years on we have poorly performing carbon markets (from the point of view of seriously reducing emissions) and other alternatives that could have been more effective have been successfully sidelined.[30]

An American commentator, Joseph Romm, pointed out in 2008 that it had taken a full decade following the 1997 Kyoto Protocol for the European Union to get a price in place, and even then coal-fired power stations were still being pursued by utilities in four EU countries. He argued that there was not sufficient time to wait another decade for the US to find out whether a cap-and-trade scheme would work there.[31]

Leaving aside the political barrier of it being a new form of taxation, a carbon tax would in principle be simpler and faster than an ETS for countries such as the US to implement. There is no doubt that a carbon tax would also be subject to the same policy uncertainty as an ETS – it is hard to guess the 'right' level at which to pitch the tax. But, critically, a carbon tax could avoid some of the problems that the ETS in New Zealand and Europe has encountered – that it is difficult for the public to understand how the ETS works and to appreciate what is really happening when free allocations (equivalent to tax exemptions) are given. The ways in which the ETS is being managed are not transparent, including the allocations of free credits and the 'buy one, get one free' concession for transport fuel suppliers and fossil-fuelled electricity generators.[32] And while units can be auctioned under an ETS, as in California, it is easier for the public to understand the idea of carbon tax revenue being fully returned to the public – for example, recycled in income tax concessions. Such a recycling mechanism would help rebuild confidence in transparent carbon pricing. This has been a very successful model in British Columbia, where it has been accompanied by steady emissions reduction (with fuel use falling 19 per cent relative to the rest of Canada) and no evident loss of economic activity (the British Columbian economy has grown slightly more than the rest of Canada).[33]

APPROACHING THE INTERNATIONAL NEGOTIATIONS

The primacy of a carbon price has been one article of faith. A rather different article of faith has been that a top-down 'global' treaty approach will be the main solution to the climate crisis. This was based on the assumption that such an approach – including a Kyoto-type United Nations-mandated reduction target – could avoid 'free riding' by self-interested countries, and offers the best chance of getting all the major players on board. But a top-down treaty approach has faced formidable obstacles in certain countries, especially the US and

Canada, and it is now clear that a voluntary pledge approach will prevail on the international stage in the run-up to Paris and beyond.[34] This is captured in the term now used for what countries pledge: 'intended nationally determined contributions', or INDCs.

As noted, New Zealand walked away from committing under the Kyoto Protocol to a second commitment period, and this damaged New Zealand's reputation. And the government's 2030 target, or INDC, to take to Paris is a weak offer, of –11 per cent (relative to 1990), an offer that is not consistent with the gravity and urgency of the climate change problem. The offer will accentuate the decline in New Zealand's reputation in the climate change arena (New Zealand already ranks forty-second of fifty-eight countries in one recent climate change performance assessment).[35] Moreover, given the lack of a tangible pathway to reducing emissions, New Zealand's offer embodies the problematic nature of the pledge and review approach: a series of weak offers can undermine the impetus towards adequate 'ambition'.

THE CASE FOR NOT WAITING FOR INTERNATIONAL AGREEMENT

There are widely differing views on the effectiveness of a top-down international agreement approach. It may be that the recent shift towards an international regime of voluntary (but 'concerted') country pledges reflects increasingly limited expectations about what international agreements can achieve. Opinions on this may reflect differing world views, as highlighted by writers on cultural theory.[36] In Europe, views appear to indicate a continuing belief that strong and binding international agreements can engender concerted action. But US opinion has long been doubtful about binding top-down approaches. The US consistently undermined the Kyoto Protocol, and US commentators still frequently dismiss it, despite the 20 per cent carbon emissions reductions the Protocol's parties succeeded in achieving.[37] This scepticism about internationally negotiated solutions is reflected in the US tradition of emphasising decentralised action.

Similarly, the late Nobel Prize-winner Elinor Ostrom pointed to *multi-level solutions* as an alternative to the internationally negotiated top-down approach. She stated:

Reliance on a single 'solution' may in fact result in more of a problem than a solution. It is important that we recognize that devising policies related to complex environmental processes is a grand challenge and that reliance on one scale to solve these problems is naïve.[38]

It may be that US thinkers have shied away from global- and national-level responses due to the political complexity and intransigence often seen at that level. But such thinkers do not always adequately confront the issue of whether a range of actions at multiple scales below the supranational – that is, national, state, country, city, local – could add up to 'going far enough, fast enough'.

The jury is out on the collective impact of sub-national action. The recent experience of regional ETSs in the US, for example, suggests that effective action at regional level is slow. The same can be said for New Zealand cities. But it may also be the case that action by cities around the world, together with regional groups, states and communities, really could add up to 'enough, in time'. Moreover, as New Zealand psychologist Niki Harré points out, individual and community-level responses are important anyway, as they engage people in a positive process of changing behaviour.[39]

In short, we do not yet know whether the voluntary-pledge, multi-level response that is on offer for the next decade will be an improvement on the limited success of the top-down approach. It may be that incentives for strong coordination and joint action remain vital. The concept of a 'climate club', an old idea with a new package, recently advocated by economists William Nordhaus and Robert Shiller, may provide a promising blueprint for this.[40]

Meanwhile, time is running out, and individual countries urgently need to prepare credible and tangible pathways to cut emissions. I next explore briefly what a small country like New Zealand might do to play a more activist role that has some chance of addressing the real challenges of climate change, focusing on energy solutions that reduce carbon emissions. I set aside the issue of New Zealand's negotiating role in international forums, reiterating only that New Zealand needs to get its domestic policy 'right' or it risks losing its remaining international credibility.[41]

As the sudden emergence of the November 2014 US–China climate policy pact suggests, things can sometimes happen fast at a high level. If the great powers decide to act and New Zealand has not done its domestic homework, it may be left behind. Only if New Zealand anticipates a global low-carbon transformation and acts accordingly can it maintain its economic competitiveness and make a substantive contribution to the international process of reducing emissions.

3. TOWARDS A GREEN ECONOMY

In considering what New Zealand can and might do, let us set aside for the moment the ethical arguments and start with the basic pragmatic case for acting to cut emissions. In the face of objections that action is costly and that New Zealand is only a bit player on the international stage, the basic arguments for action are that New Zealand can benefit in a number of different ways.

First, New Zealand can have some positive influence and encourage other nations to take action if it acts resolutely. To the extent that other nations do act, New Zealand then benefits from those actions, as the climate change risk falls. Second, there are major co-benefits in the shorter term from acting, such as the improved health of New Zealanders insulating their houses, or engaging in active travel rather than using their cars – I will investigate these more later. Third, there is an economic and social benefit of reducing the risk of having to act more precipitately in future. Fourth, New Zealand will benefit economically from maintaining its reputation as clean and green, thus assisting its trade and tourism. Last but not least, cutting emissions will give a small but direct global environmental benefit in terms of climate change damage avoided. Although New Zealand's contribution on this score will be small, the same is true for all communities of four or five million people anywhere in the world. Every contribution helps.

TECHNOFIXES

A green, low-carbon economy is *not* just about 'technofixes'. Technological advances are often held out to be the obvious solution to the climate change problem. This optimistic stance holds that breakthroughs will emerge over time as innovation proceeds, and that it is simply a matter of accelerating such fixes in order to resolve our climate change difficulties. This is attractive, as capitalism is nicely set up to offer a constant stream of marketable new technologies, and business continuity can be envisaged in such an outlook. But it relies so much on not addressing problems now and is so patently over-optimistic that, as Naomi Klein puts it, it amounts to 'looking away' from the problem.[1] I see three main objections to relying heavily on 'technofixes' as a way of addressing the climate change problem.

First, consider timing. It can be argued that most of the technologies we will in practice have – and can use on the climate change problem by 2050 – are already with us. A report from the UK Royal Academy of Engineering said recently that,

... because the timescale for the proving and large-scale roll-out of major infrastructure is measured in decades, only the low-carbon technologies that are already known can make a significant contribution to meeting the 2050 targets. They are already in the marketplace, close to it or close to being demonstrated at scale. Untried developments, such as nuclear fusion, may contribute to the energy mix beyond 2050 but to meet the 80% target we have to use what we already understand.[2]

Moreover, expert commentators such as Vaclav Smil suggest caution over time lags in deploying new energy technologies – they usually take a generation to develop and roll out. Probably the best example is carbon capture and storage (CCS), which Smil argues is essentially a pipedream in terms of tangible benefits before 2050, and would not become widely available in time to prevent CO_2 concentrations rising above 450 parts per million (a level approximately corresponding to the 2°C guardrail).[3]

Second, reliance on further technological development involves a degree of uncertainty and risk. The process is unpredictable, the technologies will inevitably have their own distinct problems, and they may well take longer than the time we have available to generate carbon benefits. The uncertainties and complexities in developing and implementing CCS are again instructive.

A variant of this objection focuses on the risky side-effects of technologies. Jared Diamond argues in his book *Collapse* that many of the problems we face are the unintended results of technology.[4] A vivid example of this is geoengineering, the notion that 'technofix' measures such as selectively scattering particles in the upper atmosphere can usefully offset global warming. Naomi Oreskes and Erik Conway neatly skewer this dangerous technological fantasy,[5] but many others have also noted that geoengineering would create a perverse effect of justifying ongoing emissions while allowing deeply problematic aspects of climate change such as ocean acidification to go unchecked. Related to this, some geoengineering measures could potentially create unintended climate disruption, such as changes to the Indian monsoon, creating migration nightmares.

Third, and most fundamentally, technologies always sit inside a social context, one in which conventions of human behaviour and norms of technology use are as important as the technology itself. A consequence is that we cannot be sure that social processes will reliably generate rapid emission reduction. The pre-eminent example is the car, which has a complex and sometimes fraught relationship with human society, as the car and society have co-evolved over time. Societies find very different ways of using the car, some emissions intensive and others less so. It is certainly possible that the developed world is well down the road to the eclipse of the car as a dominant technology, as a result of changing demographics and tastes. But car use is growing in developing countries. Optimistically, digital communication may allow the car to be used more efficiently, with car sharing, while a new generation of young people may find some appeal in less costly, and less environmentally disruptive, alternatives to the car. I discuss such changes in the transport sector later in this chapter.

Having said that the energy technologies we have now will largely dominate the period to 2050, it also has to be noted that advances in renewable energy technologies in general are very helpful. In particular, advances in environmentally sustainable technologies, such as those continuing to lower the price of solar photovoltaic (PV) power, will be essential. But they may have unintended consequences, and they take time to 'socialise', that is, for society to find ways to use them that turn out to be socially acceptable and not environmentally damaging in themselves.[6] Establishing the environmental limits on the use of hydropower technology was a process that took around a century, for instance, and we are still finding ways to balance social and environmental concerns against the benefits of wind power. Decentralised solar PV power also promises to be disruptive to the major electricity generators, as the Australian experience is showing. The debate over net metering – how much providers of decentralised solar PV power should be paid when they send power back into the grid – is an expression of this.[7]

Developing a green economy goes beyond 'technofixes' in an active and strategic attempt to find a set of technological solutions that pass tests of economic, social and environmental acceptability. For example, a green economy transport system would be one that would avoid carbon emissions, avoid polluting ambient air, encourage people to be physically active where possible, minimise the use of costly resources, and be equitable in its social impacts and provision of social opportunities. Such outcomes are not easily or quickly achieved, even if we know broadly which way we wish to head.

Lastly, in thinking about changes in energy technology, we might heed the advice of the new specialists in 'socio-technical transitions' such as

David Tyfield and Timothy Foxon.[8] Tyfield notes that there is an important place for disruptive, low-carbon technologies, especially in developing countries.[9] An example is electric bicycles, of which there are now well over 120 million on Chinese roads. Undoubtedly some of these disruptive innovations will be applied in New Zealand.

In the next section, I set out some elements of a low-carbon energy transformation for New Zealand, as a part of a wider green economy vision. This vision is one that includes the fostering of green research and the creation of green jobs.

A GREEN ECONOMY ENERGY TRANSITION

Some limited empirical evidence is available on how a transition to low-carbon energy might progress in New Zealand. Of course, there is no 'right' scenario: we can decide to shape the future, or respond rather passively to how the world evolves. New Zealand has tended to do the latter in recent years, but there is a strong case for doing the former if we are to have a liveable New Zealand in the long term. I offer examples of findings and initiatives in three vital transition arenas: the phasing out of energy subsidies, tackling the tough nut of transport energy use, and targeting 100 per cent renewable energy.

Phasing out energy subsidies

Internationally, New Zealand takes a principled stance on subsidies, no doubt conscious of the evidence that energy subsidies are responsible for a great deal of waste and unnecessary carbon emissions. Fatih Birol, chief economist of the IEA, estimated in January 2012 that '37 governments spent $409 billion on artificially lowering the price of fossil fuels in 2010'.[10] The subsidies significantly lift oil and gas consumption and disadvantage renewable energy technologies, which by contrast received only $66 billion of subsidies in the same year. Birol is reported to argue that cuts in subsidies could provide around *half* the emissions reductions needed over the next decade to reach a trajectory limiting warming to 2°C.

Despite New Zealand's principled stance on subsidies, domestic energy subsidies in New Zealand do exist. Given the plethora of 'unburnable' reserves of fossil fuels internationally,[11] there is no case for New Zealand taxpayer support to the oil and gas industry, mainly as a tax deduction for petroleum-mining expenditures.[12] Another current energy subsidy is given by the New Zealand government to the smelter at Tiwai Point, which takes around 12 per cent of the country's total electricity at an undisclosed but low price. The closure of the smelter, although necessitating transition assistance for some workers, would be a welcome potential contributor to a sustainable energy transition. It is estimated that it would lower wholesale electricity prices by 10 per cent for some years.[13] The case for closing the smelter will strengthen if aluminium prices weaken further. Already there are strong reasons to doubt the logic of using 600 megawatts, a valuable slice of renewable electricity capacity, on the production of an energy-intensive commodity in falling demand.

To the extent that alternative production facilities are now often more energy efficient, in nations such as China, emissions would likely fall as production moved offshore. New Zealand can re-route the electricity through an upgraded national grid to other users, so that job losses in Southland (which has low unemployment) would be offset by job and economic gains elsewhere in New Zealand. Smelter closure and reduced demand for new generation would also likely bring forward the full closure of the old Huntly coal-powered station, further reducing New Zealand's emissions.

Lower-carbon transport
A range of encouraging opportunities for more sustainable transport is coming into view. Three critical areas are the development of electric vehicles (EVs), the resurgence of active travel (walking and cycling), and using digital connectivity to leverage urban intensification into easy access

and more attractive urban lifestyles. These are all linked.

Electric mobility (electric cars, buses, cycles) is likely to be a major element in the energy (and transport) transition. It is reasonable to project a continued reduction in the cost of production of battery power, which currently constitutes over half the cost of battery-driven electric cars. One international study suggests electricity could provide 44 per cent of transport energy by 2050, with 70 per cent of that transport energy from renewables.[14] Tony Seba of Stanford University is more optimistic, seeing essentially all new mass-market motor vehicle sales in the US by 2030 as being EVs and also autonomous (self-driving) or semi-autonomous.[15]

A New Zealand study envisages that almost 400,000 EVs could be on the road by 2025, requiring only another 180 megawatts of electricity system capacity.[16] Overall carbon emissions could be cut, due to reduced tailpipe emissions, by 1.5 to 3 million tonnes per year by 2040.[17] Similarly, cautious modelling by New Zealand government agencies concludes that EVs may become more widely available and reasonably competitive by around 2030, but significant take-up will depend on oil and carbon prices going considerably higher. This may or may not occur in the next decade with the growth in unconventional oil production.

Douglas Clover has carried out extensive modelling of EV take-up in New Zealand and has integrated his vehicle fleet modelling with an electricity-generation system model to simulate impacts on power production.[18] His work suggests that a carbon price of the sort earlier discussed in this text – such as NZ$100 per tonne of CO_2 – combined with high EV take-up could by 2030 reduce CO_2 emissions from the light passenger vehicle fleet and the electricity-generation sector together by up to 45 per cent, depending on the scenario assumed for the expansion of electricity generation. High rates of EV take-up would almost certainly require some form of government encouragement, such as support for recharging infrastructure. Clover's study also found that recharging of EVs should be undertaken largely off-peak in order to minimise the construction of new power stations.

It is important to remember, however, that EV production itself (including battery production) is about twice as carbon intensive as conventional internal combustion engine vehicle production, and about half of an EV's lifetime carbon footprint comes from its production.[19] This means that in Europe, for example, EVs may come out only 10–30 per cent ahead of conventional vehicles in terms of carbon emissions, although New Zealand's largely renewable electricity increases the advantage relative to the European situation. At the same time, production of EVs is currently more environmentally damaging than production of normal internal combustion vehicles, in terms of human toxicity, ecosystem toxicity and particulate matter formation.[20] And, of course, EVs do nothing to reduce traffic congestion, and may even adversely affect safety in cities.

A more fundamental transformation of vehicle energy use, and a corresponding carbon emissions reduction, would follow from more active travel in cities. A recent Dutch cycling expert visiting Christchurch commented that Christchurch could be the world's cycling capital, in part because it is flat and spacious.[21] Many other New Zealand cities such as Nelson, Whanganui, Hastings and New Plymouth could also be cycling-intensive cities, and in some cases have made a good start in this direction. In Hastings and New Plymouth, the Model Communities Programme, an active travel infrastructure and education programme, has been found to successfully arrest the decline in cycling that would otherwise have taken place.[22] While the fuel savings from leaving the car at home will not initially be large, they may grow significantly if cycling rates rise. At the same time, the substantial co-benefits for health arising from cycling are very important.[23] Along with conventional cycling for health, use of electric bikes for longer or hillier trips is becoming more attractive as the range of e-bikes on offer improves and prices fall.[24]

A third important and related element is improved digital connectivity. Young people with smart phones appear more willing to use public transport and to walk as this does not disrupt their connections but rather can enhance opportunities for extended listening or conversations. Glenn Lyons has suggested that this trend, which is evident in the flattening of 'vehicle kilometres travelled' profiles in a range of developed countries,[25] may be pushing the car into a position as a 'background functional technology', not the technology that has dominated so much of our society in recent years.[26] Commentators such as Kingsley Dennis and John Urry make a similar point. They question the way western culture has privileged the car and moulded the ways we live and move in its favour, and point to major emergent changes.[27] One example is bike-sharing schemes, now implemented in nearly 700 cities. Another is car sharing. There were over 1 million members of such schemes in North America in early 2013.[28]

Digital connectivity growth and policies to support bike- and car-sharing schemes – together with proximity assisted by more compact urbanisation and a changing demographic profile of society (especially with more older people) – may help significantly in reducing vehicle kilometres travelled and thus carbon emissions. Moreover, if we as a nation are persuaded that it is desirable to move in this lower-carbon direction, and policies are shaped to support this outcome, there is every reason to think it will occur.[29]

100 per cent renewable energy

It is also worth considering whether New Zealand would be blazing an altogether pioneering trail if it set its sights on 100 per cent renewable energy. New Zealand at present is about 80 per cent renewable in terms of *electricity* (2014 data), and about 39 per cent renewable in terms of total *primary energy* supply.[30] New Zealand could readily get to 100 per cent renewable electricity (save for gas peaker plants in the short term), and indeed go beyond this: electricity could start to substitute for fossil fuels in a number of areas of energy use, such as motor vehicles.

Denmark, a country in many ways similar to New Zealand, and with an even longer record of minority governments, has a target of 35 per cent renewable *energy* by 2020 (that is, *below* New Zealand's current level), but 100 per cent by 2050. The Danish Energy Agency estimates, as noted earlier, that the costs of this ambitious commitment will 'work out at EUR 1 per day per household over the next 40 years'.[31] Given the greater diversity of New Zealand's renewable energy endowment compared to Denmark's, there is reason for New Zealand to be just as ambitious as Denmark, aiming at 100 per cent renewable *electricity* by 2025 and 100 per cent renewable *energy* by 2050. The sticking point will likely be those industries such as steel making and milk processing, in which large quantities of process heat are needed, and freight transport, where there are no adequate substitute energy sources at present. Because of this, and to allow time for new technologies and practices to emerge, 100 per cent renewable energy would need to remain an aspirational target at this stage.

How much confidence should New Zealanders have in the development and implementation of new energy technologies? A key conclusion from high-level studies of various energy innovations – from CCS (discussed earlier in the chapter) to solar power – is that technological transitions take time to mature. What are called 'sustainability transitions' in the literature are likely to take even longer, as solutions tend to be more complex than just a move to the next profit-making technology.[32]

One conclusion in a US study is that the gap between new research and technology break-throughs and widespread development is usually a matter of decades, but there are – encouragingly – some areas of new, more sustainable technology such as wind energy and PV where the upturn in patents has foreshadowed, with a relatively short (five- to seven-year) gap, the upturn in technology rollout.[33] But in terms of widespread adoption of new technologies, energy expert Vaclav Smil cautions that 'energy transitions … are inherently prolonged affairs whose duration is measured in decades or generations, not in years'.[34] In New Zealand there is considerable uncertainty over how long grid-tied PV electricity prices may take to reach grid parity,[35] but recent dramatic international price reductions in PV suggest it might be only a few years.[36]

Would a high price on carbon accelerate the transition to new technologies in New Zealand? One recent New Zealand study looked at whether a substantial carbon price would significantly affect certain energy-investment decisions.[37] The study examined electricity storage/reserve generation options, clearly an issue in the local context, where there is increasing availability of intermittent wind and (eventually) solar power, but people still wish to have a reliable enough power supply to be able to turn on their heat pumps at peak hours such as 6 p.m. on a winter's night.

The study found that pumped hydro was seen by most experts in the sector as prohibitively costly (as well as environmentally difficult), even if it was technically capable of providing renewables support and peak-power adequacy. Utility-scale batteries were seen as not currently cost effective, with very high storage costs per kilowatt-hour (1 kilowatt of power expended for one hour); they would most likely be used in New Zealand only for very high-value applications where there is a strong technical advantage, such as the six-second instantaneous reserve. But the key point is that a price on carbon of around NZ$100 per tonne of CO_2 was seen as making these technologies much more competitive; that is, climate change mitigation policy was seen as a strong driver of possible take-up of these storage options.

Of course, investment decisions about reserve generation are only one aspect of the electricity market that would be influenced by a high carbon price. It is also interesting to examine recent modelling data on energy generation under a significant carbon price, namely, a $100 per tonne scenario. Overall, the Ministry of Economic Development (the forerunner of the present Ministry of Business, Innovation and Employment) concluded that such a price (assumed in that scenario to be reached by 2020 and then held) would generate a 7 per cent fall in total energy emissions.[38] But there would be significantly different impacts in different energy sectors, for example:

- petrol-transport demand would fall only 0.8 per cent relative to the reference ($25 per tonne) scenario

- wind generation would increase 80 per cent and coal generation would fall by 36 per cent, and
- electricity prices would rise by 8 per cent.

It would be optimistic to say that New Zealanders would welcome these changes, but they might be palatable if the energy security and other benefits of renewables investment were well explained.

It is beyond the scope of this essay to assess the scope for social and behavioural change in the transport sector. However, the estimates just given of the low proportional impact of a carbon price in the transport sector indicate the challenge of changing behaviour in this sector, especially in the short run. Currently, work is going on in areas such as active transport promotion,[39] along with studies of changes in the configuration of cities and the likely impact this may have on carbon emissions over time.[40] It is important that this work is accelerated and deepened.

4. MOTIVATING RAPID ACTION

Before a green economy vision can take hold, New Zealanders need to understand the case for collective action toward that vision. Here I first examine some evidence on New Zealanders' (and, for comparison, Americans') awareness and thinking about climate change action. Then I discuss a policy mix that might appeal more widely than a policy directed solely at climate change.

AWARENESS AND COMMITMENT: A TIPPING POINT?

How prepared are New Zealanders to act, or do they feel powerless and immobilised by the climate change problem? This is important to know in order to gauge how prepared New Zealand politicians and the public would be to accept policies necessary for major changes in everyday energy and transport practices.

In a May 2014 pre-election survey of New Zealanders aged fourteen and over, only 1 per cent mentioned climate change or global warming as the most important problem facing New Zealand; and only 6 per cent rated it the most important problem facing the world.[1] While this suggests a low awareness of the wider ramifications of climate destabilisation, the 'most important' formulation of the question is problematic, and earlier and deeper surveys gave a more nuanced picture.

In a fairly typical 2009 poll, for example, about 43 per cent of 500 respondents saw climate change as a serious or very serious concern, but this concern was lower than that expressed about education, health, the cost of living and most other nominated issues.[2] Climate change ranked eighth of nine issues. When asked whether humans are having an impact on world climate patterns, 22 per cent rated human impact on climate as 4 or less on a 10-point scale, whilst 41 per cent rated humans as having a very direct impact on climate, that is, 8–10 on the scale. So, considerably more New Zealanders (than not) viewed human impacts as significant. This result is similar to that of another nationwide survey that found 38 per cent of the New Zealand public strongly believe (9 or 10 on a 1–10 scale) that humans or animals have a direct impact on climate change.[3]

In a 2013 poll limited to environmental issues, 21 per cent of respondents identified climate change as the single biggest issue facing the world, but it was seen as sixth most important for New Zealand after water pollution and some other pollution issues.[4]

This cluster of results shows that while a majority of New Zealanders are generally aware of humans' impact on climate change, with almost as many viewing it as a serious concern, they tend to see it as less important than other environmental issues for New Zealand. This also suggests that they are not seeing the connections between global climate disruption and flow-on impacts for New Zealand.

What about views on climate *policies*? The 2009 poll just mentioned found a small majority supported an ETS if costs imposed were not high.[5] The Business Council for Sustainable Development commissioned polls over the 2007–10 period that suggested that 65–76 per cent of New Zealanders believe that climate change is a problem to be dealt with 'now' or 'urgently'.[6] This concern subsequently weakened: a 2012 Horizon poll found that the proportion of New Zealanders regarding climate change as an urgent or immediate problem had declined to 52.4 per cent (from 75.4 per cent in 2008).[7] On carbon pricing, the same poll found 28.2 per cent of respondents supported carbon pricing, while 28.7 per cent opposed it (31.7 per cent were neutral on the issue, and 11.4 per cent did not know).[8]

A Wellington region study found that 70 per cent reported that they had taken action in relation to climate change, and – perhaps not surprisingly – those who saw the risks of climate change as high were more likely to have taken action. The question 'How soon should climate change be dealt with?' elicited a mean score of 4.3 on a 1–5 scale, suggesting a sense of urgency. This study also found that when asked about the commons dilemma (for example, 'Feeling that other individuals will not change their actions even if I do'), respondents did not indicate that the dilemma had much influence on their behaviour (mean scores on the three questions about the commons dilemma were 2.8 on a 1–5 scale). Similarly, when asked about whether a sense of powerlessness influenced their behaviour, respondents' scores indicated relatively little influence (mean 2.7 on a 1–5 scale).[9]

An important insight for shaping policy on climate change mitigation comes out of the evidence just mentioned about New Zealanders' political priorities. It is clear that New Zealanders place great weight on *health* services and health outcomes compared to many other priorities, including economic growth.[10] This suggests that more joining of the dots between climate change mitigation and health benefits needs to be undertaken. Put negatively, health outcomes will clearly be threatened in a world with an unstable and more extreme climate, as many health specialists have underlined. Put positively, carbon mitigation policies can create health and quality-of-life gains. The emphasis needs to be on the *co-benefits* of policy measures, such as the health benefits of active travel, better quality housing and living more centrally in compact cities.[11] Some groups, such as OraTaiao (the New Zealand Climate and Health Council), and individuals are working in this vein;[12] and the World Health Organization's (WHO's) work on this theme is invaluable.[13] This is not to say that the co-benefits will necessarily fully compensate for the cost of some climate policies. But they will undoubtedly help people to see that tackling climate change is not necessarily a matter of cost and sacrifice – there are quality-of-life benefits from the lower-carbon lifestyles that can replace aspects of today's carbon-intensive patterns of living.

How do New Zealanders view technological and behavioural solutions to the carbon-mitigation issue? We have little evidence about behavioural change, but we have some evidence on attitudes to the challenge of transforming New Zealand's energy system to, say, 100 per cent renewable electricity. For example, some evidence suggests New Zealanders are very positive about clean-energy technologies and tend to be optimistic about technological solutions to environmental issues. For example, an Energy Efficiency and Conservation Authority-commissioned 2008 survey by AC Nielsen found that 86 per cent of New Zealanders surveyed were supportive of wind farms in New Zealand,[14] and a Business Council for Sustainable Development survey found that most New Zealanders (77 per cent and 69 per cent) preferred wind and solar electricity generation respectively to gas (10 per cent).[15] However, whether and to what extent wind power or another form of power generation is supported by particular communities is much more complex, and depends on the size of the power development and the local site, as well as environmental, institutional and economic factors.[16]

What I conclude provisionally from this patchwork of evidence is that New Zealanders on the whole do want to be active on climate change, and they are likely to favour policies that have co-benefits in terms of other goals such as health, quality of life, energy security and – very likely – long-term economic gain, arising, for example, from enhancing New Zealand's clean, green reputation.

The difficulties of raising public awareness need to be borne in mind. Some in the business sector will continue to see climate change policies as threatening to their particular livelihoods and offering few positives in terms of enhancing their chances of employment. Business people in New Zealand have tended to oppose carbon pricing or at best to be neutral rather than supportive,[17] and particular groups such as the Business Roundtable have played a key role in delaying policy action over the last quarter-century, as evidenced in the film *Hot Air: Climate Change Politics in New Zealand*.[18] But many other business people see the need for action,[19] and it is notable how positive the New Zealand union movement has already been, judging by the stance of the New Zealand Council of Trade Unions.[20] There are many examples from the Scandinavian social democratic experience that speak to livelihood concerns.[21]

It is also worth remembering that attitudes in New Zealand are often influenced by foreign opinion and, increasingly, the media in countries such as the US, UK and Australia. As attitudes change overseas, we tend to see change percolating into New Zealand thinking.[22] Because of its large influence on New Zealand opinion, it is worthwhile having a quick look at US opinion on climate change.

First, there is a large gap in the US between the public and climate scientists.[23] For example, among the public in the late 2000s, 58 per cent agreed that 'human activity is a significant contributing factor in changing mean global temperatures', while among climate scientists, who (one assumes) understand long-term climate processes, agreement was 97 per cent.[24] Despite this deficit in the US public's awareness or knowledge, it is notable that a substantial majority of the US public have for some time wanted the government to do more about climate change.[25] But little action has eventuated.

One explanation is that for most Americans climate change is a low priority. A 2011 poll of policy priorities for the US government found that 'respondents put dealing with climate change second-to-last out of 22 options'.[26] The 'climate silence' noted in the 2012 US election campaign by a number of journalists supports this finding;[27] rather than a serious discussion of climate policy, the presidential candidates vied to explain how they would extract more fossil fuels to keep fuel prices down for Americans. Since that election campaign the big increase in fossil-fuel extraction in the US has helped to drive down global oil and gas prices, confirming expectations. On the other hand, a recent (January 2015) poll found that an overwhelming majority of Americans, including half of Republicans, now support government action to curb climate change.[28] It is possible that President Obama's positioning and actions on climate change, and a growing sense of extreme climate impacts, have contributed to changing opinion in the US. It is possible also that a developing bandwagon effect – a shift in consciousness referred to by some as a 'climate swerve' – could be rapidly reflected in New Zealand sentiment.[29] There are some early indications of such a trend in the US.[30]

It is sobering that Berkeley's George Lakoff argues that modern liberal democracies are suffering from a problem of embedded conservative framing and engrained worldviews that require a fundamental challenge, and that embedding a more progressive set of frames is a desirable but long, probably decadal, process. As he states:

What is needed is a constant effort to build up the background frames needed to understand the [environmental] crisis, while building up neural circuitry to inhibit the wrong frames. That is anything but a simple, short-term job to be done by a few words or slogans.[31]

The prospects for education about climate change are positive in the medium term. But for education to make a major difference to climate change, it has to influence opinion and filter through to policy-makers in the next decade or so. This seems ambitious. In terms of both awareness raising and education, the task of transforming the way people think about climate- and energy-related behaviour is non-trivial and needs to be accelerated.

IMPLICATIONS FOR A NEW ZEALAND STRATEGY

The New Zealand picture sketched here of a range of technological and policy options, and a public reasonably sympathetic to (but not yet convinced by) mitigation action, suggests that some of the building blocks are in place for transformative change, but not all. Gaps include vision and a strategy for handling resistance.

New Zealand presently lacks a credible, coherent vision for an active transition to a green, low-carbon economy. This will need a clear framing narrative and explanation. It is interesting that a recent Royal Society of Edinburgh review of climate change policy found that the biggest barrier to a low-carbon Scotland was the 'lack of coherence and integration of policy at different levels of governance'.[32] Among their recommendations, for example, were that 'local authorities should integrate and embed their low-carbon policies across all their various functions', and that 'the Scottish Government and local authorities should actively assist local communities to introduce low-carbon initiatives'.

A strategy for a low-carbon transition is likely to encounter obdurate resistance from specific interests such as the oil, gas and coal industry, the pro-fracking fossil-fuel community, roading contractors and suburban-housing developers, and more diffuse resistance from those more generally lacking awareness of the dizzying rate of change of the science and projected impacts of climate change.[33]

Some well-off individuals in New Zealand, who are most likely responsible for a disproportionate share of household emissions, may not relish reining in their emissions.[34] This resistance can be seen in terms of the theory of cultural cognition – those with an interest in the status quo, whose cultural values are reinforced by their peer group, are reluctant to change their behaviour in the face of changing scientific information.[35] This framework may help to explain not just the resistance of big emitters but also the resistance of other groups to change. Such resistance will have to be addressed carefully by central and local government, working with communication experts and others, to raise understanding of the enormity of the risks associated with climate change and fossil-fuel use, to reframe the narratives of change and to look for acceptable policy solutions.

New Zealand's low-carbon energy transition will need a mix of mutually reinforcing policies, as each policy measure will by itself be inadequate to make much of an impact in moving to a plausible low-carbon emission trajectory. Each policy measure also has its difficulties and costs, and the lead times are often long. Providing alternative transport choices, for example, is a multi-year investment process. Such 'complementary' policies (that is, complementary to a price on carbon) are critical in enabling change. They must be worthwhile in themselves, having direct benefits and co-benefits that are clear and positive. But they also facilitate responses to price signals.

Recognising that a high carbon price is a long political stretch in the short term, complementary policies have a critical role in preparing the way for a rising carbon price. Transitioning to a meaningful carbon price – a level of around $100 per tonne, the sort of price suggested by Nicholas Stern – is an important short-term policy goal. Its logic is that such a price signal is highly effective because it is a pervasive re-orientation of diverse parts of the economy. It aligns well with complementary policies that prepare the way by creating 'enabling conditions'. Revenue recycling is essential in making a rising price politically more palatable. In my view, the approach would be simpler, more understandable and more trusted if the price was to take the form of a transparent revenue-neutral tax rather than an opaque ETS price, but both price instruments allow revenue recycling.

As argued earlier, complementary measures need to be *multi-level* policies, involving central, regional and local government, and also involving households and individuals. As outlined above, they need to cover energy, transport and cities, at the minimum.

Cities are critical for the medium to long term. Looking across cities, there is evidence that carbon emissions are negatively (and with strong statistical significance) correlated with city population density. That is, denser cities emit less carbon per capita, mainly because trip distances are shorter. Higher density is also associated with mixed land use (diversity of activity). And emissions also rise with economic activity (but not sharply) and fall with petrol prices (significantly). Indeed, a recent estimate is that urban form, economic activity, transport costs and geographic factors explain 88 per cent of urban transport energy use.[36] So what local government does to shape the form of our cities matters – and is a strong determinant of energy use and carbon emissions over time, even if changing these patterns is not a quick fix.

At present the ability of cities to mitigate carbon emissions is heavily constrained. Even if they support a higher carbon price they cannot implement one, as this is a central government prerogative. Nor, even where they wish to have more investment in walking, cycling and public transport (rather than catering for motor vehicles), can they control road funding, largely a central government call. Minimal provision has been made by central government for active travel support and this situation has discouraged active travel investment by cities in the last few years. Where it has occurred, in New Plymouth and Hastings, for example, it has been shown to be effective in countering the trend away from cycling in such cities. However, with the recent small increment of central government funding for cycling ($100 million over four years, or about 1 per cent of road funding) announced in the 2014 election campaign, prospects for active travel in cities are significantly improving.

While such change is helpful, cities remain constrained. The central government insistence (since an amendment in 2004) that the Resource Management Act 1991 (RMA) exclude consideration of mitigating climate change (although not the *effects* of climate change) is not consistent with a multi-level enabling approach, where cities and regional councils take mitigation into account in planning. There is a good case for amending the RMA in this respect, given the current political inhibition about raising the price of carbon.

New Zealand cities are increasingly committed advocates of a green economy, expressed in different ways. Auckland, for example, seeks to be 'the world's most liveable city: a quality, compact city', and this informs its proposed Unitary Plan under the RMA. In Wellington, the 2040 vision of Wellington City Council also sets a green economy aspiration. In both cases, these cities are aiming to establish reputations that will appeal to skilled and talented migrants.

A green economy strategy appeals to our most prosperous cities and represents a credible alternative model in the eyes of the OECD, WHO and others.[37] If anything, a green economy is being questioned as insufficiently radical by some in the international debate, who ask whether ongoing economic growth can be sustained under *any* regime in the long term.[38] It is curious, then, that green economy policies seem to have no current appeal to New Zealand's central government. The current economic track, although it is accommodating some increase in renewable electricity generation, risks embedding an outdated extractive economic model and fossil-fuel dependent infrastructure, especially in transport and the industrial sectors.[39] The current government has nodded in the direction of green growth but done little to date; the report of the Green Growth Advisory Group was largely left to wither on the vine.[40]

New Zealand can expect the international trend towards economic greening to gather momentum, as countries emerge from the current period of economic difficulty and as awareness grows of the negative impacts and risks of unmitigated climate change. Investment in greening the economy, especially the energy sector, is also likely to help sustain progressive sectors in other economies as they transition to a greener model.[41] There is huge potential for New Zealand to be a front-runner in this transition, especially given its renewable energy resources, flexible economy and innovative, educated population. Equally, there is potential to miss out on this transformative process.

Coherence in terms of vision, messaging and awareness-building is a vital part of a New Zealand low-carbon, green economy transition. There are some early signs of alignment between: enlightened members of the business sector;[42] social enterprise organisations such as the Ākina Foundation; progressive local government; 'green' non-governmental organisations (NGOs) such as OraTaiao, 350.org.nz and Generation Zero; and the academic community, including groups such as the New Zealand Centre for Sustainable Cities, the Centre for Sustainability and even the Royal Society of New Zealand.[43] All these sectors and organisations understand the need to raise awareness about the risks of climate change and the need to keep the pressure on for a green economy transition with strong carbon mitigation.

5. THE RISKS TO BALANCED GOVERNANCE

Given the urgency and pervasiveness of climate change, the transformational challenge is a combination that some have called 'wicked' (or even 'super wicked').[1] With such problems, there is no easy or popular answer; they are a difficult combination of the need to overcome policy and public attention fatigue, maintain motivation in the face of economic and other distractions, and handle deliberate political resistance, including from some less visionary businesses and parts of the establishment.[2] If the mitigation delays of the last decade, due in part to the global financial crisis, are repeated, or there are further delays because of factors such as the difficulty of significantly lifting the global carbon price in the face of political opposition, then moving past the 2°C guardrail becomes almost inevitable.

There is always a risk in democracies of self-defeating pessimism, especially on a complex international issue such as climate change. Consider US public opinion. A poll was conducted in late 2011/early 2012 of over 2,000 US adults.[3] The poll divided Americans into six groups, from the 'dismissive' (10 per cent) to the 'alarmed' (13 per cent). Majorities of the 'alarmed', 'concerned', 'cautious' and 'disengaged' said that humans are capable of reducing global warming, but that it is 'unclear at this point' whether humans will 'do what's needed'. Between 20 and 27 per cent of all the groups except the 'dismissive' believed that humans could reduce global warming, but 'are not going to do so because people aren't willing to change their behaviour'. Only 6 per cent or less in each of the six groups felt humans will 'successfully reduce global warming'. These numbers suggest there is a danger of pessimistic thinking setting in – a self-fulfilling prophecy effect.[4]

So many Americans are inclined to think that humans will *not* 'do what's needed' about climate change that little might end up being done. This view may be entrenched if Americans selectively focus on China's *growth* in fossil-fuel emissions (207 per cent over 1990–2009 versus 7 per cent in the US) and ignore the US's much greater carbon footprint per capita – 17 tonnes in 2009 versus China's 5 tonnes.[5]

The limited public understanding of climate change mentioned earlier could prove highly problematic for informed democratic decision-making on climate change. Consider the finding of a survey conducted at the 2010 Cancun climate summit, among 500 accredited attendees from around the world. This found that 94 per cent agreed that 'without strong public support, real action on climate change will never be made at the international governmental level' and 'when asked what constituencies need to be more involved, respondents ranked the general public number one, ahead of heads of state, business, NGOs and UN organizations'. Some 58 per cent said that 'the general public does not understand the meaning of "climate change" well or at all', and only 5 per cent said the public understands it 'very well'.[6] In short, those at the international negotiations are looking to the public for a lead, while frequently the converse is also true – the public look to governments and the international negotiations for a lead. In this sense, the climate policy dog is chasing its tail.

Some degree of pessimism about collectively solving the climate change problem is also prevalent in other democracies such as Canada, Australia and Japan, where current administrations seem to be moving backwards on climate policy. A trenchant critique of Prime Minister Harper's Canadian policies has pointed out that Canada will now not even come close to meeting the lax emission reduction target that it promised in 2009 when it announced its withdrawal from the Kyoto Protocol. Also worryingly, the Canadian government appears to have cut climate change research funding and is fighting anti-tar-sands environmental groups.[7] And in Australia, while Mr Abbott has had to retreat from his 'strategically ignorant' statements about climate change, including his view that climate change science is 'crap',[8] his contrarian views still, at time of writing, hold sway. Fortunately, Mr Abbott is increasingly out of step with Australian public opinion: for example, a poll in December 2014 found that 57 per cent of all respondents believed the Coalition's proposed Direct Action policy was 'too little' to deal with global warming.[9]

As we witness growing climate destabilisation over the next decade, we may well see growth in the movement to rethink the conventional wisdoms of the present generation and establishment, such as the primacy of economic growth at the expense of its underpinning support system, the biosphere. One unlikely convert in his thinking is Robert Rubin, a former Treasury secretary under President Clinton. He formerly argued that the Kyoto Protocol would damage the US economy, but more recently stated:

[Climate change is] the existential threat of our day ... Once you see it as having catastrophic impact, any economic argument follows that, because you're not going to have an economy [if you don't deal with climate change].[10]

Rubin and other business leaders in the US are involved in the 'Risky Business' initiative aimed at raising awareness among business people, on the basis that their interests will be dramatically damaged by unmitigated climate change. It can be hoped that this will have broad appeal in most parts of the US, save perhaps for a few such as Wyoming, where legislators say 'teaching climate change could hurt the local economy'.[11]

Climate change is increasingly seen as too important to be left to scientists, or to economists to 'optimise'.[12] The conventional policy approach of analysing mitigation action in an economic framework, based on apparently careful assessments of costs and benefits of climate change abatement, is increasingly seen to be inappropriate or ill-judged, as Rubin's comment suggests. Partly this is because Nicholas Stern, Simon Dietz and other eminent economists have questioned standard assumptions about climate damage.[13] They point out how quickly our understanding of the complex atmosphere–biosphere interactions is being overturned by new information, suggesting greater damage is possible. But it is also because people are often unhappy with making judgements about climate policy on the basis of an economic cost–benefit trade-off; they see the issue equally as an ethical one on which people have diverse perspectives.[14] Moreover, as one US economist argues, we now need to 'focus on avoiding the worst, rather than obtaining the optimal'.[15]

It is not surprising that many young people reject many of the assumptions and conclusions of the 'baby boomer' generation now in power, a generation that is reluctant to challenge its own assumptions. Generation Zero, for example, wants to see a new focus on radical policy change to solve the problem of climate change within one generation. One generation is, of course, the timeframe for resolution that climate change now forces upon us.[16] As recently underlined by Nicky Hager, young people in New Zealand can be underestimated.[17] There is evidence that they do more or less understand the nature of the climate change crisis and – importantly – are not likely to be demotivated or daunted by the scientific realities or brutal honesty about the size of the policy and behavioural challenge, as long as they see a positive way forward. As David Roberts, a US commentator, put it:

There's no reason that intensity, activism, protest, and agitation – 'alarmism', as they're snottily called by Very Serious People – need to be seen as an *alternative* to pragmatic, incremental process pushed by moderate insiders ... But everyone, it seems to me, no matter what role they play, could stand to push the edge a little bit occasionally, reminding their audience, whatever audience, that climate change is some genuinely dire sh*t and that now is the time for ambition and courage.[18]

A similar notion was voiced by financier Jeremy Grantham, writing in the top journal *Nature* in 2012. He entitled his article 'Be persuasive. Be brave. Be arrested (if necessary)', and argued that it was 'crucial that scientists take more career risks and sound a more realistic, more desperate, note on the global-warming problem'.[19]

However, there is a darker risk, a potential connection between creeping climate destabilisation and loss of democratic capacity to take action and to cope with adaptation. A decade ago, New Zealand geologist Peter Barrett argued that warming of 3°C would risk 'the end of civilisation as we know it'; his judgement was based on three decades of research into the past 40 million years of Antarctic climate.[20] Leaving aside the paleo data, is there a more immediate supporting argument and evidence that civilisation itself is at stake ?

Evidence is beginning to connect climate shocks to civil conflict. For example, Solomon Hsiang and colleagues found a doubled probability of new civil conflicts arising in the tropics during El Niño years relative to La Niña years.[21] The US Joint Forces Command recognises the significance of climate change as a risk intensifier, arguing that natural catastrophes exacerbated by climate change can pose severe threats to weak states.[22]

In our own lifetimes we are increasingly given glimpses into the economic, social and political breakdown that scorching drought and extreme storm events are likely to engender in countries from Russia to India and the US. Given that less than 1°C of global warming can currently send an estimated 56 per cent of the US into drought and extreme temperatures, to cite 2012 data, and unleash damaging coastal flooding, 3°C or more of warming would bring much greater intensity of destabilisation. As Angel Gurría, the head of the OECD, recently stated, we are currently on course for 3–5°C, and this is 'betting the planet'.[23]

And recent extreme events in Asia allow us more readily to imagine the disruptive effect of perhaps 20 million refugees (one estimate of the number at risk by 2100) moving within or beyond Bangladesh in anticipation of, or in crisis-mode response to, increased flooding, storm events and loss of agricultural land near the coast. While it is unclear exactly how climate change will play out, increased flooding, drought and growing-season disruption impacting on food prices could lead to political crises in a wide swath of countries, including some of the more vulnerable small island states close to New Zealand.

All or most of the land in Kiribati, Tokelau, Tuvalu and Tonga is low lying (much is currently within 1 metre of sea level) and at risk of storm surge and salt water intrusion with rising sea levels. As these countries come under stress with climate change, there will be intensifying political pressure for New Zealand initially to provide adaptation funds, and then to accept immigrants and provide the resources to support resettlement. Learning from other countries, it is clear that absorbing tens of thousands of climate refugees is unlikely to be politically easy, and it will be wiser for New Zealand governments to face and manage the problems earlier rather than wishing them away.

A complicating factor in any society's ability to keep taking democratic action, and to stay resilient, is a potential breakdown in consensus. Alongside the lag in people's understanding of the extent of the climate change problem, we have seen some increased polarisation – what some call the entrenching of climate change as part of a 'culture war'. As the public has become more worried that solving climate change may require drastic lifestyle changes, the issue has become more polarised. For some time conservatives in the US preferred to focus on combating the growing scientific evidence on climate change, with an anti-democratic tendency during the Bush years to try to suppress some of the evidence and water down scientific conclusions. There was a worrying crackdown on outspoken scientists such as Jim Hansen.[24] Andrew Hoffman, writing in the US, says:

... there appears to be a deepening schism between the skeptical and convinced logics, one that rests on foundational arguments that are based on different worldviews, different issues, and different frames to communicate them.[25]

In short, there is not yet a strong social consensus in the US, nor in a few other developed countries, on climate change, and particularly not on the means to tackle it. For the delicate process of cooperative decision-making under time pressure, polarisation is a profound problem.

Rather than convincing the 'unready', crisis conditions could undermine the building of consensus about major social and economic policy choices. It is difficult, even without the pressure of urgency, to agree on the direction of social and economic development. As one observer argues, 'above 2°C of warming, any notion of development rather than merely a process of damage limitation will be lost ...'.[26] It is inevitable that the damage-limitation problem and social polarisation will be much more extreme if warming exceeds 3°C.

And if warming were to continue to 4°C, climate expert Kevin Anderson describes that future as 'incompatible with any reasonable characterisation of an organised, equitable and civilised global community'.[27]

A significant change in the Indian monsoon could precipitate huge instability on the Indian subcontinent, for example, especially if it coincided with the sort of Russian grain embargo seen in 2010.[28] In a political environment of instability and uncertainty, international cooperation – such as it currently is – could be dangerously diminished, contributing to international inertia, political stalemate and an extended, worsening climate crisis.[29]

We can expect that economic and political uncertainty associated with intensifying climate change will erode the flexibility and even stability of democracies, from India to the US, and from the Netherlands to New Zealand. At times of instability it is notoriously difficult for governments to look outwards, to take long-term sustainable decisions that protect future generations and minority interests, and even to maintain freedoms. People under stress tend to turn inwards and reach for simple solutions that offer apparent stability, while trying to protect shorter-term interests and their own narrow community. Clive Hamilton writes eloquently about this human proclivity:

The success of climate denialism in its various guises reveals how shallow are the roots of the Enlightenment … In the most vital test of our capacity to protect the future through the deployment of rationality and well-informed foresight, the 'rational animal' is manifestly failing. We see now that the forces unleashed by science and the commitment to a rational social order had entered into a contingent alliance only.[30]

The Tea Party-influenced trajectory of the US right wing suggests this is beginning to happen today. The 2012 US election campaign featured Mitt Romney mocking President Obama for even thinking of trying to mitigate climate change. Romney, noting with irony that 'President Obama promised to begin to slow the rise of the oceans, and to heal the planet', pledged instead to 'help you and your family'. The pitch was to step back from action on climate change and pander to narrow self-interest. While the Republicans cry that 'The most powerful environmental policy is liberty',[31] it appears that liberty is being reframed as the freedom to ignore climate destabilisation.

Fortunately, something of a backlash has developed in the US against extreme polarising propaganda. The Heartland Institute in May 2012 ran a very short-lived billboard campaign mocking 'belief' in global warming, associating it with the 'Unabomber', Ted Kaczynski. But the Institute had to cancel the campaign when a number of objecting donors withdrew their funding. While the climate deniers in the US have not gone away, since superstorm Sandy they fortunately seem to be on the back foot, and some may be reconsidering the rationality of their position.

Other observers have noticed a connection between instability and poor governance. The Davos World Economic Forum's report on Global Risks 2015 notes:

Global risks transcend borders and spheres of influence and require stakeholders to work together, yet these risks also threaten to undermine the trust and collaboration needed to adapt to the challenges of the new global context.[32]

New Zealand is, of course, not immune to poor governance during times of crisis. Although our democracy appears robust at present, periods of authoritarian repression such as the treatment of conscientious objectors in the First World War and dissenters during the 1951 waterfront dispute should give us pause. At other moments since the Second World War, there have been reasons for doubt about our government and its links to more powerful others, as portrayed, for example, in C. K. Stead's novel *Smith's Dream*. It is not difficult to imagine a McCarthyist crackdown, or another brand of authoritarianism, bolstered by the tools of mass surveillance, at a future moment when the economy is in shock from repeated climate events and import supply lines are under threat as international trade is disrupted.

History warns us to be on the alert for an erosion of balanced governance and democracy in the face of crisis, and a time of burgeoning climate change is not likely to be conducive to rational and progressive ideas and reform. Such dire developments are not inevitable at this point. But consideration of the possibilities and scenarios is warranted. It brings us full circle to the timing issue: the speed with which the storm is gathering leaves little time for complacency or half-hearted action if we are to retain a democratic future. We need a full-bodied response, now.

6. ACTING WHILE WE STILL HAVE TIME

Destabilisation of the world's climate system is accelerating and could soon become irreversible, not just within our lifetimes but within a decade or two. It is not an exaggeration to report that some natural systems such as the Greenland ice sheet are already on the cusp of irreversible change. Setting aside the matter of tipping points in the climate, it is worth registering that well before the end of this century the phenomena of extreme heat and drought over large parts of the Earth will make life intolerable for many. Disruption to the New Zealand economy and way of life caused by drought, storms, flooding and other extreme events will be an increasing risk. A key indicator of whether the problem is under control is progress to hold global warming to under 2°C, the guardrail on which countries agreed as recently as 2009 in Copenhagen. The chances of holding global warming below this threshold are increasingly slim. In short, the stakes are enormous – and time is running out.

This is not just an environmental and economic issue, although there are important economic and other consequences to climate destabilisation. It is, more importantly, a political-ethical issue. Is it fair to future generations to sleepwalk into climate instability, essentially for a very temporary extension of this generation's current prosperity? Is this a rational and wise way to manage our resources and our precious and unique civilisation?

There are technological and policy solutions available or emerging, and – for most countries – they centre on changes to energy systems, broadly interpreted. I have focused on those. (For New Zealand, measures to reduce agricultural greenhouse gases and encourage forestry are also important, but are not covered in this essay, because of the complexity of the debate around the carbon cycle and living systems and because, ultimately, CO_2 matters most.) In addition to emission reductions in New Zealand's energy system, linked changes to our transport systems and urban form and design can also contribute to cutting emissions.

While urgent, the necessary changes in our energy system would not be excessively expensive, especially compared to the damage that climate destabilisation will cause. Moreover, many policy measures would yield co-benefits – health gains, for example. But sustained policy and behavioural change is needed. For New Zealand, a policy target of 100 per cent renewable *electricity* within a decade (by 2025) is achievable, and 100 per cent renewable *energy* by 2050 may also be achievable and is worth aiming for. A positive focus on such goals could galvanise all parts of society into contributing to the management of climate change and would showcase New Zealand's clean, green credentials internationally.

Changes to our local energy systems will require rapid policy change and a mix of well-aligned policies across a wide range of sectors, but they are doable. Contrary to the impression that may be created by the international negotiation process, effective action across international, national and local levels is not dependent on the outcome of negotiations. And contrary to the conventional wisdom of economists, necessary changes are unlikely to be achieved by a price on carbon alone, although a substantial and rising price, preferably in the form of a carbon tax with fully recycled revenue, would help a lot. Nor are individual behaviour changes sufficient. Big changes to our energy system – our patterns of energy production and consumption – need to go beyond individual behavioural actions and require collective public policy action.

Given the gaps in public understanding of the climate threat, a critical part of the political action needed is to increase awareness through public education, including education about the nature of the threat of climate change. Equally, a critical part of the solution is for our democratic leaders to listen to the action measures that the progressive majority of people would like to see put in place. But this will not be enough. Nor is better coordinated governance, even though it is important. It is essential for effective change that careful attention is given by governments and the informed public to the ways in which the issues are framed, particularly ensuring that solutions are framed in positive terms, while explaining the co-benefits of action and effectively communicating a positive vision. Ideally, we would see wide public discussion and a broad consensus on a low-carbon, green economy strategy, with a vision and pathway for each sector. This will not be easy to achieve, especially as it may need to be developed against a disruptive background of creeping climate destabilisation.

As the climate change threat grows, the incentive for action will increase, but the remaining opportunity for democratic decision-making about rational climate policy is likely to diminish steadily.

The dark side of climate destabilisation is the threat it poses to rational and balanced governance, and democratic policy-making, even in New Zealand. This is perhaps the most critical argument of all for urgent action.

It has been observed many times that humans are not good at responding to threats that are distant in time and space.[1] Many people prefer to ignore early warning signs of climate instability and crisis, thus risking an even more extreme crisis in future.[2] As George Monbiot has eloquently put it, climate change seems to be 'a catastrophe we are capable of foreseeing but incapable of imagining …'.[3]

It is vital, however, also to be aware of the positive side, which many people are. Like commentator George Marshall, I assess the situation as being far from hopeless.[4] Rapid shifts in public attitudes, and government motivation to take policy action, are not only possible but also plausible in the near future.

This essay has explored what can be done in a time of useful consciousness. We can use this brief interlude to good effect. New Zealand and New Zealanders are in a strong position to take action and exert positive international influence through that action. But we need to act very smartly, in both senses of the word, or we shall lose the race to act in time.

LIST OF ACRONYMS

CCS	carbon capture and storage
CDM	'Clean Development Mechanism' (Kyoto Protocol)
ETS	emissions trading scheme
EU	European Union
EV(s)	electric vehicle(s)
IEA	International Energy Agency
INDC	'intended nationally determined contributions'
IPCC	Intergovernmental Panel on Climate Change
MED	Ministry of Economic Development
MfE	Ministry for the Environment
MIT	Massachusetts Institute of Technology
NGO(s)	non-governmental organisation(s)
OECD	Organisation for Economic Co-operation and Development
PV	photovoltaic (power)
RMA	Resource Management Act 1991
UN	United Nations
WHO	World Health Organization

NOTES

Introduction

1   R. Gifford, 'The Dragons of Inaction: Psychological Barriers That Limit Climate Change Mitigation', *American Psychologist*, 66, 4 (2011), pp.290–302.

2   P. Krugman, 'Gambling with Civilization', *New York Review of Books*, 7 November 2013, pp.14–18.

3   C. Shaw, 'The Dangerous Limits of Dangerous Limits: Climate Change and the Precautionary Principle', *The Sociological Review*, 57, s2 (2009), pp.103–23.

4   D. Sarewitz, 'Science and Environmental Policy: An Excess of Objectivity', Consortium for Science, Policy and Outcomes, Arizona State University, 2000.

5   J. Cook et al., 'Quantifying the Consensus on Anthropogenic Global Warming in the Scientific Literature', *Environmental Research Letters*, 8, 024024 (2013).

6   P. H. Gleick, R. M. Adams, R. M. Amasino et al., 'Climate Change and the Integrity of Science', *Science*, 2010, pp.689–90.

7   N. Oreskes and E. M. Conway, 'Global Warming Deniers and Their Proven Strategy of Doubt', *Yale Environment*, 360 (2010).

8   I am indebted to my daughter Amy Howden-Chapman, drawing on Lawrence Ferlinghetti, for this insight: see ndbooks.com/book/time-of-useful-consciousness (accessed 13 July 2015).

Chapter 1

1   New Zealand Climate Change Research Institute, K. Trenberth, 'The Russian Heat Wave and Other Recent Climate Extremes', Wellington, 2011.

2   The World Bank, The International Cryosphere Climate Initiative, 'On Thin Ice: How Cutting Pollution Can Slow Warming and Save Lives', Washington DC, 2013.

3   IPCC, 'Climate Change 2013: The Physical Science Basis, Summary for Policymakers', Working Group I Contribution to the IPCC Fifth Assessment Report, 2013.

4   Munich Re, '2013 Natural Catastrophe Year in Review', 7 January 2014.

5   G. M. Heal and A. Millner, 'Agreeing to Disagree on Climate Policy', *Proceedings of the National Academy of Sciences*, 111, 10 (2014).

6   T. Wei, S. Yang, J. C. Moore et al., 'Developed and Developing World Responsibilities for Historical Climate Change and CO_2 Mitigation', *Proceedings of the National Academy of Sciences*, 109, 32 (2012), pp.12911–15; M. New, D. Liverman, H. Schroder and K. Anderson, 'Four Degrees and Beyond: The Potential for a Global Temperature Increase of Four Degrees and its Implications', *Philosophical Transactions of the Royal Society A: Mathematical, Physical and Engineering Sciences*, 369, 1934 (2011), pp.6–19.

7   K. Anderson and A. Bows, 'Beyond "Dangerous" Climate Change: Emission Scenarios for a New World', *Philosophical Transactions of the Royal Society A: Mathematical, Physical and Engineering Sciences*, 369, 1934 (2011), pp.20–44; J. Hansen, M. Sato and R. Ruedy, 'Climate Variability and Climate Change: The New Climate Dice', 2011; K. Blok, N. Höhne, K. van der Leun and N. Harrison, 'Bridging the Greenhouse-gas Emissions Gap (Commentary)', *Nature Climate Change*, 2, 7 (2012), pp.471–74.

8   P. Friedlingstein, S. Solomon, G. K. Plattner, R. Knutti, P. Ciais and M. R. Raupach, 'Long-term Climate Implications of Twenty-first Century Options for Carbon Dioxide Emission Mitigation', *Nature Climate Change*, 1, 9 (2011), pp.457–61.

9   K. Anderson and A. Bows, 'A New Paradigm for Climate Change', *Nature Climate Change*, 2, 9 (2012), pp.39–40.

10 A. Robinson, R. Calov and A. Ganopolski, 'Multistability and Critical Thresholds of the Greenland Ice Sheet', *Nature Climate Change*, 2, 6 (2012), pp.429–32.

11 S. Goldenberg, 'Western Antarctic Ice Sheet Collapse Has Already Begun, Scientists Warn', *The Guardian*, 12 May 2014, www.theguardian.com/ environment/2014/may/12/ western-antarctic-ice-sheet- collapse-has-already-begun- scientists-warn (accessed 5 July 2015).

12 D. Pollard, R. DeConto and R. Alley, 'Potential Antarctic Ice Sheet Retreat Driven by

Hydrofracturing and Ice Cliff Failure', *Earth and Planetary Science Letters*, 412, 15 February (2015), pp.112–21.

13 The World Bank and The International Cryosphere Climate Initiative, 'On Thin Ice'.

14 R. G. Prinn, 'Development and Application of Earth System Models', *Proceedings of the National Academy of Sciences*, 110, s1 (2012).

15 B. Hare, M. Rocha, M. Schaeffer et al., 'China, US and EU Post-2020 Plans Reduce Projected Warming: Climate Action Tracker Policy Brief', Climate Analytics, Potsdam Institute for Climate Impacts Research, Ecofys and NewClimate Institute, 2014.

16 D. Coumou and A. Robinson, 'Historic and Future Increase in the Global Land Area Affected by Monthly Heat Extremes', *Environmental Research Letters*, 8, 034018 (2013).

17 N. Oreskes and E. M. Conway, 'The Collapse of Western Civilization: A View from the Future', *Daedalus*, 142, 1 (2013), pp.40–58.

18 Robert Rubin, 'How Ignoring Climate Change Could Sink the U.S. Economy', www.washingtonpost.com (accessed 5 July 2015).

19 McKinsey & Company, 'Pathways to a Low-carbon Economy: Version 2 of the Global Greenhouse Gas Abatement Cost Curve', New York, 2009.

20 IEA, 'World Energy Special Outlook Report: Redrawing the Energy-Climate Map', Paris, 2013.

21 O. Tsukimori and R. Kebede (eds), 'Japan on Gas, Coal Power Building Spree to Fill Nuclear Void', www.reuters. com/article/2013/10/16/ us-japan-power-outlook-idUSBRE99F02A20131016 (accessed 5 July 2015).

22 IEA, 'World Energy Outlook', Paris, 2011.

23 US Council of Economic Advisers, 'The Cost of Delaying Action to Stem Climate Change', Washington DC, 2014.

24 J. Hansen, 'Climate Change is Here — and Worse Than We Thought', *Washington Post*, 4 August 2012.

25 H. Stewart and L. Eliot, 'Nicholas Stern: "I Got It Wrong on Climate Change – It's Far, Far Worse"', *The Guardian*, 26 January 2013, www.theguardian.com/ environment/2013/jan/27/

nicholas-stern-climate-change-davos (accessed 5 July 2015).

26 M. Weitzman, 'Fat-Tailed Uncertainty in the Economics of Catastrophic Climate Change', presented at the REEP Symposium on Fat Tails, Harvard University, 23 February 2011.

Chapter 2

1 K. Anderson and A. Bows, 'Reframing the Climate Change Challenge in Light of Post-2000 Emission Trends', *Philosophical Transactions of the Royal Society A*, 366, 1882 (2008), pp.3863–82. See also K. Anderson and A. Bows, 'A New Paradigm for Climate Change', *Nature Climate Change*, 2, 9 (2012), pp.39–40.

2 E. Martinot, 'REN21, Renewables Global Futures Report 2013', Paris, 2013; The Global Calculator, 'Prosperous Living for the World in 2050', insights from uncached-site. globalcalculator.org (accessed 5 July 2015).

3 Geoff Bertram and Simon Terry, *The Carbon Challenge: New Zealand's Emissions Trading Scheme*, Bridget Williams Books, Wellington, 2010; R. Garnaut, *The Garnaut Review 2011*, Cambridge University Press, Melbourne, 2011.

4 A. Kaletsky, *Capitalism 4.0*, Bloomsbury, London, 2010.

5 J. Roper, 'Environmental Risk, Sustainability Discourses, and Public Relations', *Public Relations Inquiry*, 1, 1 (2012), pp.69–87.

6 Pure Advantage, 'New Zealand's Position in the Green Race', Auckland, 2012.

7 I. Davison, 'Climate Swings Donor Left', *New Zealand Herald*, 15 April 2014, www.nzherald.co.nz/ nz/news/article.cfm?c_ id=1&objectid=11238187 (accessed 5 July 2015).

8 A. Gurría, 'Climate: What's Changed, What Hasn't and What We Can Do About It – Six Months to COP21', lecture by Angel Gurría, Secretary-General, OECD, 3 July 2015, London, www.oecd.org/about/ secretary-general/climate-what-has-changed-what-has-not-and-what-we-can-do-about-it.htm (accessed 13 July 2015).

9 The World Bank, 'Turn Down the Heat: Why a 4°C Warmer World Must Be Avoided', Report by the Potsdam Institute for Climate Impact Research and Climate

Analytics, Washington DC, 2012.

10 B. Metz, 'The Legacy of the Kyoto Protocol: A View from the Policy World', *Wiley Interdisciplinary Reviews: Climate Change*, 4, 3 (2013), pp.151–58.

11 T. Baird, 'Fossil Fuel Independence: Denmark's Path', *IEA Energy The Journal of the International Energy Agency*, 2 (Spring 2012), p.41.

12 O. Lucon, D. Ürge-Vorsatz, Ahmed A. Zain et al., 'Buildings', in O. Edenhofer, R. Pichs-Madruga, Y. Sokona et al. (eds), *Climate Change 2014: Mitigation of Climate Change. Contribution of Working Group III to the Fifth Assessment Report of the Intergovernmental Panel on Climate Change*, Cambridge University Press, Cambridge and New York, 2014, pp.671–738.

13 Treasury, '2014 Briefings to Incoming Ministers', Information Release Document, Wellington, 2014.

14 F. Ackerman and E. Stanton, 'Climate Risks and Carbon Prices: Revising the Social Cost of Carbon', Economics for Equity and the Environment Network (E3), Portland, 2011; C. Hope, 'The Social Cost of Carbon: What Does it Actually Depend on?', *Climate Policy*, 6 (2006), pp.5656–572.

15 W. Nordhaus, 'Economic Aspects of Global Warming in a Post-Copenhagen Environment', *Proceedings of the National Academy of Sciences*, 107, 26 (2010), pp.11721–26; S. Howes, F. Jotzo and P. Wyrwoll, 'Nordhaus, Stern, and Garnaut: The Changing Case for Climate Change Mitigation', Crawford School of Economics and Government, Australian National University, Canberra, 2011; Interagency Working Group on Social Cost of Carbon, United States Government, 'Technical Update of the Social Cost of Carbon for Regulatory Impact Analysis', Washington DC, 2013.

16 K. Than, 'Estimated Social Cost of Climate Change Not Accurate, Stanford Scientists Say', *Stanford Report*, Palo Alto, 2015.

17 F. C. Moore and D. B. Diaz, 'Temperature Impacts on Economic Growth Warrant Stringent Mitigation Policy', *Nature Climate Change*, 2015; Y. Cai, K. L. Judd, T. M. Lenton et al., 'Environmental Tipping Points Significantly Affect the

Cost–Benefit Assessment of Climate Policies', *Proceedings of the National Academy of Sciences*, 112, 15 (2015).

18   A. Macey, 'Climate Change: Towards Policy Coherence', *Policy Quarterly*, 10, 2 (2014), pp.49–56.

19   In granting permission to reproduce Figure 1, the Ministry for the Environment supplied a list of caveats and requested they be included in this publication. Their caveats are listed here without any editing:

'(i) This graph shows projections of net emissions under the current second Commitment Period Kyoto Protocol accounting rules which are applicable to the 2013-2020 period only. In contrast, the UNFCCC net emissions shown in the 6NC graph apply consistent rules that are applicable over the whole time series. (ii) Under Kyoto Protocol rules, accountable net emissions start from the first commitment period (2008), therefore estimated net emissions over 1991-2007 are included for illustrative purposes only. Different Kyoto Protocol accounting rules apply for the 2008-2012 and 2013-2020 commitment periods. (iii) Countries are negotiating a new international climate change agreement to apply to all countries from January 2021. The accounting settings for commitments have yet to be agreed under this future agreement, including for net emissions (incorporating forestry and land-use). This uncertainty makes it difficult to quantify New Zealand's future net emissions and removals after 2020. The post-2020 projections should be treated with caution, are potentially misleading, and are illustrative only. (iv) All estimates and projections are subject to ongoing revision and recalculation as per internationally agreed good practice, and may no longer be current. Estimates and projections of emissions and removals are calculated differently for New Zealand's GHG reporting under the UNFCCC and the Kyoto Protocol. Please see New Zealand's GHG Inventory report for an explanation of these differences. (v) The projections of net emissions reflect a mid-range emissions and removals scenario based on multiple assumptions regarding economic behaviour and other drivers of emissions, and should be treated with caution. It is important to note that these projections are inherently uncertain and use the current low carbon price. (vi) Uncertainty in emissions projections increase over time, and projections should be treated with extreme caution beyond 2030. (vii) No account is taken of the surplus Kyoto Protocol units that New Zealand holds and will use to meet its CP1 target and unconditional 2020 target.'

20 Ibid., pp.49–56; B. Fallow, 'A Year On, Climate Policy Still a Disgrace', *New Zealand Herald*, 19 December 2013, www.nzherald.co.nz/business/news/article.cfm?c_id=3&objectid=11174771 (accessed 5 July 2015).

21 Bertram and Terry, *The Carbon Challenge*.

22 MfE, 'New Zealand's Fifth National Communication under the United Nations Framework Convention on Climate Change', Wellington, 2009.

23 Ministry of Economic Development (MED), 'New Zealand's Energy Outlook 2011: Reference Scenario and Sensitivity Analysis', Wellington, 2011.

24 MfE, 'Environmental Stewardship for a Prosperous New Zealand: Briefing to the Incoming Ministers', Wellington, 2014.

25 M. Rocha, B. Hare, J. Cantzler et al., ' New Zealand Deploys Creative Accounting to Allow Emissions to Rise: Climate Action Tracker Policy Brief', Climate Analytics, Potsdam Institute for Climate Impacts Research, Ecofys and NewClimate Institute, Berlin, 2015, s3.documentcloud.org/documents/2164199/nz-indc-assessment-july-2015-embargo.pdf (accessed 17 July 2015).

26 M. Weitzman, 'Fat-Tailed Uncertainty in the Economics of Catastrophic Climate Change', presented at the REEP Symposium on Fat Tails, Harvard University, 23 February 2011.

27 MfE, 'New Zealand's Sixth National Communication under the UNFCCC and the Kyoto Protocol', Wellington, 2013.

28 MED, 'New Zealand's Energy Outlook 2011'; MfE, 'Questions and Answers on New Zealand's 2020 Emissions Reduction Target', Wellington, 2009.

29 J. Wright, 'Submission on the Climate Change Response (Emissions Trading and Other Matters) Amendment Bill [September]', Parliamentary Commissioner for the Environment, Wellington, 2012.

30 E. Boyd, M. Boykoff and P. Newell, 'The "New" Carbon Economy: What's New?', *Antipode*, 43, 3 (2011), pp.601–11.

31 J. Romm, 'Cleaning Up On Carbon', *Nature Reports Climate Change*, 2008.

32 B. Fallow, 'NZ Ducking the Climate Question', *New Zealand Herald*, 21 November 2014, www.nzherald.co.nz/business/news/article.cfm?c_id=3&objectid=11361890 (accessed 5 July 2015).

33 S. Elgie, R. Beaty and R. Lipsey, 'British Columbia's Carbon Tax Shift: An Environmental and Economic Success', blogs.worldbank.org/climatechange/british-columbia-s-carbon-tax-shift-environmental-and-economic-success (accessed 5 July 2015).

34 F. Pearce, 'Dangerous Decade: What Follows the Durban Climate Deal', *New Scientist*, 13 December 2011; A. Macey, 'The Road to Durban and Beyond: The Progress of International Climate Change Negotiations', *Policy Quarterly*, 8, 2 (2012), pp.23–28; H. D. Jacoby and Y.-H. Henry Chen, 'Expectations for a New Climate Agreement', MIT Joint Program on the Science and Policy of Global Change, Cambridge, MA, 2014.

35 J. Burck, F. Marten and C. Bais, 'The Climate Change Performance Index Results 2014', Bonn, 2014, germanwatch.org/en/7677 (accessed 13 July 2015).

36 M. Verweij, M. Douglas, R. Ellis et al., 'Clumsy Solutions for a Complex World: The Case of Climate Change', *Public Administration Review*, 84 (2006), pp.817–43.

37 Metz, 'The Legacy of the Kyoto Protocol'.

38 E. Ostrom, 'A Multi-Scale Approach to Coping with Climate Change and Other Collective Action Problems', *Solutions*, 1, 2 (2010), pp.27–36.

39 Niki Harré, '*Psychology for a Better World: Strategies to Inspire Sustainability*', Auckland, 2012.

40 R. Shiller, 'How Idealism, Expressed in Concrete Steps, Can Fight Climate Change', *New York Times*, 27 March 2015, www.nytimes.

com/2015/03/29/upshot/
how-idealism-expressed-in-
concrete-steps-can-fight-
climate-change.html (accessed
5 July 2015).

41 Macey, 'Climate Change'.

Chapter 3

1 N. Klein, *This Changes
Everything*, Simon and
Schuster, New York, 2014.

2 Royal Academy of Engineering,
'Generating the Future: UK
energy systems fit for 2050',
London, 2010.

3 V. Smil, 'Global Energy: The
Latest Infatuations', *American
Scientist*, 99 (2011), pp.212–19.

4 J. Diamond, *Collapse*, Penguin
Books, London, 2005.

5 N. Oreskes and E. M. Conway,
'The Collapse of Western
Civilization: A View from
the Future', *Daedalus*, 142, 1
(2013), pp.40–58.

6 S. Jasanoff, 'A New Climate
for Society', *Theory, Culture
& Society*, 27, 2–3 (2010),
pp.233–53.

7 R. Chapman, 'The Way to Go?
American or German Solar
Incentive Models', *Solar Action
Bulletin*, SAB94 (June 2013),
pp.8–9.

8 T. J. Foxon, 'A Coevolutionary
Framework for Analysing a
Transition to a Sustainable

Low Carbon Economy',
Ecological Economics, 70, 12
(2011), pp.2258–67.

9 D. Tyfield, J. Jun and T. Rooker,
'Game-changing China (1)'
and 'Game-changing China
(2)', www.chinadialogue.net/
article/show/single/en/3704-
Game-changing-China-1- and
www.chinadialogue.net/
article/show/single/en/3704-
Game-changing-China-2 (both
accessed 5 July 2015).

10 D. Clark, 'Fossil Fuel Subsidies:
A Tour of the Data', *The
Guardian*, 19 January 2012,
www.theguardian.com/
environment/datablog/2012/
jan/18/fossil-fuel-subsidy
(accessed 5 July 2015).

11 J. Leaton and B. Ward,
'Unburnable Carbon 2013:
Wasted Capital and Stranded
Assets', Carbon Tracker & The
Grantham Research Institute,
London School of Economics,
2013.

12 World Wildlife Fund New
Zealand, 'Fossil Fuel Finance
in New Zealand, Part 1:
Government Support',
Wellington, 2013.

13 Treasury, 'New Zealand
Aluminium Smelters (NZAS)
Information Release,
T2012/1470: Project 14: Initial
Advice', Wellington, 2013.

14 S. Teske, J. Muth and S. Sawyer, 'Energy [R]evolution: A Sustainable World Energy Outlook', Greenpeace International, European Renewable Energy Council, Global Wind Energy Council, Amsterdam, 2012.

15 Tony Seba, *Clean Disruption of Energy and Transportation*, Palo Alto, 2015, www.TonySeba.com (accessed 13 July 2015).

16 J. Duncan, T. Halliburton, B. Heffernan et al., 'Electric Vehicles: Impacts on New Zealand's Electricity System', Centre for Advanced Engineering New Zealand, Christchurch, 2010.

17 Ibid.

18 D. Clover, 'The Market for Electric Vehicles in New Zealand: Using Stated Choice Methods to Evaluate the Implications for Electricity Demand and Carbon Emissions to 2030', presented at the VUW GED Seminar Series, Victoria University of Wellington, 1 August 2013.

19 T. R. Hawkins, B. Singh, G. Majeau-Bettez and A. H. Strømman, 'Comparative Environmental Life Cycle Assessment of Conventional and Electric Vehicles', *Journal of Industrial Ecology*, 17, 1 (2012), pp.53–64.

20 Ibid.

21 A. Tukia, 'Christchurch Could be Cycling Capital', interviewed on TV3, *3News*, Christchurch, 2014.

22 R. Chapman, P. Howden-Chapman, M. Keall et al., 'Increasing Active Travel: Aims, Methods and Baseline Measures of a Quasi-experimental Study', *BMC Public Health*, 14, 1 (2014), pp.935–47; M. Keall, R. Chapman, P. Howden-Chapman et al., 'Increasing Active Travel: Results of a Quasi-experimental Study of an Intervention to Encourage Walking and Cycling', *Journal of Epidemiological and Community Health*, 2015, in review.

23 G. Lindsay, A. Macmillan and A. Woodward, 'Moving Urban Trips from Cars to Bicycles: Impact on Health and Emissions', *Australian and New Zealand Journal of Public Health*, 35, 1 (2011), pp.54–60; B. Giles-Corti, S. Foster, T. Shilton and R. Falconer, 'The Co-benefits for Health of Investing in Active Transportation', *New South Wales Public Health Bulletin*, 21, 6 (2010), pp.122–27.

24   J. MacArthur, J. Dill and M. Person, 'E-Bikes in North America: Results from an Online Survey', 93rd Annual Meeting of the (US) Transportation Research Board, January 2014.

25   P. Newman and J. Kenworthy, '"Peak Car Use": Understanding the Demise of Automobile Dependence', *World Transport, Policy & Practice*, 17 (2 June 2011).

26   G. Lyons, 'The Future of Transport', futureagenda.org, London, 2014, www.futureagenda.org (accessed 13 July 2015).

27   K. Dennis and J. Urry, *After the Car*, Polity Press, Cambridge, 2011.

28   The Global Commission on the Economy and Climate, 'Better Growth, Better Climate: The New Climate Economy Report', World Resources Institute, Washington DC, 2014.

29   G. Lyons, C. Davidson, T. Forster et al., 'Future Demand: How Could or Should Our Transport System Evolve in Order to Support Mobility in the Future?', Ministry of Transport, Wellington, 2014.

30   MED, ' New Zealand Energy Data File: 2011 Calendar Year Edition', Wellington, 2012.

31   T. Baird, 'Fossil Fuel Independence: Denmark's Path', *IEA Energy The Journal of the International Energy Agency*, 2 (Spring 2012), p.41.

32   A. Bergek, S. Jacobsson, B. Carlsson et al., 'Analyzing the Functional Dynamics of Technological Innovation Systems: A Scheme of Analysis', *Research Policy*, 37, 3 (2008), pp.407–29.

33   A. Rau, R. Toker and J. Howard, 'Can Technology Really Save Us From Climate Change?' *Harvard Business Review*, 88, 1 (2010), pp.21–23.

34   V. Smil, 'Global Energy'.

35   M. Watt, 'Assessment of the Future Costs and Performance of Solar Photovoltaic Technologies in New Zealand ACT, Australia', IT Power Australia Pty Ltd and Southern Perspectives Ltd, 2009.

36   US Department of Energy, '$1/W Photovoltaic Systems: White Paper to Explore A Grand Challenge for Electricity from Solar', Advanced Research Projects Agency, 2010.

37   G. Kear and R. Chapman, 'Reserving Judgement: Perceptions of Pumped Hydro and Utility-Scale Batteries

for Electricity Storage and Reserve Generation in New Zealand', *Renewable Energy*, 57 (2013), pp.249–61.

38 MED, 'New Zealand's Energy Outlook 2011'.

39 R. Chapman, P. Howden-Chapman, M. Keall et al., 'Evaluating the Model Communities Programme: Literature, Methodology and Some Preliminary Results', presented at 2WALK andCYCLE Conference, Hastings, 22–24 February 2012.

40 R. Chapman, 'Transitioning to Low-carbon Urban Form and Transport in New Zealand', *Political Science*, 60, June (2008), pp.89–98.

Chapter 4

1 Roy Morgan Research, 'Economic Issues are the Most Important Problems Facing New Zealand (44%) as New Zealand Heads Towards a September Election', n = 990, Auckland, 2014.

2 D. Stuart, 'Survey on Public Attitudes to Climate Change and the Emissions Trading Scheme', Greenhouse Policy Coalition, Wellington, 2009.

3 TNS Conversa and the New Zealand Institute of Economic Research, 'Emissions Trading Scheme (ETS) Research: National Survey (Quantitative): A Summary of Quantitative Research amongst the General Public', n = 1,003, Auckland, 2008.

4 K. Hughey, G. Kerr and R. Cullen, 'Public Perceptions of New Zealand's Environment: 2013', n = 2,200, EOS Ecology, Christchurch, 2013.

5 Stuart, 'Survey on Public Attitudes to Climate Change'.

6 ShapeNZ, 'ShapeNZ Environmental Issues Survey 2010', New Zealand Business Council for Sustainable Development, Auckland, 2010.

7 Horizon Research, '22% Slump in Climate Change Concern', n = 2,829, Auckland, 3 August 2012.

8 Horizon Research, 'Public Deeply Split on Carbon Pricing', Auckland, 24 August 2012.

9 C. Aitken, R. Chapman and J. McClure, 'Climate Change, Powerlessness and the Commons Dilemma', n = 192, *Global Environmental Change*, 21, 2 (2011), pp.752–60.

10 E. Rose, J. Huakau and S. Casswell, 'Economic Values: A Report from the New Zealand Values Study, 2005', Centre for Social and Health Outcomes

Research and Evaluation &
Te Rōpū Whāriki, Massey
University, Auckland, 2005;
Growth and Innovation
Advisory Board, 'Research
Summary: Research on Growth
and Innovation', Ministry
of Research, Science and
Technology, Wellington, 2004.

11 P. Howden-Chapman and
R. Chapman, 'Health Co-
benefits from Housing-related
Policies', *Current Opinion in
Environmental Sustainability*,
4, 4 (2012), pp.414–19.

12 P. Howden-Chapman, R.
Chapman, A. G. Capon and
N. Wilson, 'Carbon Pricing is
a Health Protection Policy',
Medical Journal of Australia,
195, 6 (2011), pp.311–12.

13 WHO, 'Health in the Green
Economy: Health Co-benefits
of Climate Change Mitigation
– Transport Sector', Geneva,
2011; WHO, 'Health in the
Green Economy: Health Co-
benefits of Climate Change
Mitigation – Housing Sector',
Geneva, 2011.

14 Energy Efficiency and
Conservation Authority, 'Wind
Energy', Wellington, n.d.

15 New Zealand Business Council
for Sustainable Development,
'New Zealanders' Choice
of Future Energy Sources',
Wellington, 2008.

16 J. B. Graham, J. R. Stephenson
and I. J. Smith, 'Public
Perceptions of Wind Energy
Developments: Case Studies
from New Zealand', *Energy
Policy*, 37, 9 (2009), pp.3348–
57; M. Barry and R. Chapman,
'Distributed Small-Scale Wind
in New Zealand: Advantages,
Barriers and Policy Support
Instruments', *Energy Policy*, 37
(2009), pp.3358–69.

17 Horizon Research, 'Public
Deeply Split on Carbon
Pricing'.

18 *Hot Air: Climate Change
Politics in New Zealand*,
documentary by A. Barry and
A. King-Jones, Vanguard Films,
New Zealand, 2014.

19 Sustainable Business Council,
'Vision 2050 – The Report:
Business as Usual is Not an
Option, Auckland, 2012; Pure
Advantage, 'New Zealand's
Position in the Green Race',
Auckland, 2012.

20 New Zealand Council of
Trade Unions, 'Towards
Sustainability: Unions and
Climate Change', Wellington,
2007.

21 N. Klein, *This Changes
Everything*, Simon and
Schuster, New York, 2014.

22 R. Chapman, 'Ideas Percolate
Slowly into New Zealand',

Future Times, 4, 2 (2002), pp.3–5.

23 W. R. L. Anderegg, J. W. Prall, J. Harold and S. H. Schneider, 'Expert Credibility in Climate Change', *Proceedings of the National Academy of Sciences*, 107, 27 (2010), pp.12107–9.

24 P. T. Doran and M. K. Zimmerman, 'Examining the Scientific Consensus on Climate Change', *Eos, Transactions American Geophysical Union*, 90, 3 (2009), p.22.

25 T. L. Brewer, 'US Public Opinion on Climate Change Issues: Implications for Consensus-building and Policymaking', *Climate Policy*, 4, 4 (2004), pp.359–76.

26 E. M. Markowitz and A. F. Shariff, 'Climate Change and Moral Judgement', *Nature Climate Change*, 2, 4 (2012), pp.243–47.

27 D. Roberts, 'Climate Silence: It's the Right, Stupid', grist. org, 22 October 2012, grist.org/ politics/climate-silence-its-the-right-stupid (accessed 13 July 2015).

28 C. Davenport and M. Connelly, 'Most Republicans Say They Back Climate Action, Poll Finds', *New York Times*, 30 January 2015.

29 R. J. Lifton, 'The Climate Swerve', *New York Times: Sunday Review*, 2014.

30 Davenport and Connelly, 'Most Republicans Say They Back Climate Action'.

31 G. Lakoff, 'Why It Matters How We Frame the Environment', *Environmental Communication*, 4, 1 (2010), pp.70–81.

32 The Royal Society of Edinburgh, 'Facing up to Climate Change: Breaking the Barriers to a Low-carbon Scotland', Edinburgh, 2011.

33 R. Maetzig, 'Report Industry Spin – Greens', *Taranaki Daily News*, 8 November 2012, www.stuff.co.nz/taranaki-daily-news/news/7920818/ Report-industry-spin-Greens (accessed 5 July 2015).

34 C. Brand and B. Boardman, 'Taming of the Few:The Unequal distribution of Greenhouse Gas Emissions from Personal Travel in the UK', *Energy Policy*, 36, 1 (2008), pp.224–38.

35 D. M. Kahan, H. Jenkins-Smith and D. Braman, 'Cultural Cognition of Scientific Consensus', *Journal of Risk Research*, 14, 2 (2011), pp.147–74.

36 F. Creutzig, G. Baiocchi,

R. Bierkandt et al., 'Global Typology of Urban Energy Use and Potentials for an Urbanization Mitigation Wedge', *Proceedings of the National Academy of Sciences*, 112, 20 (2015).

37 WHO, 'Health in the Green Economy: Transport Sector'; M. Jacobs, 'Green Growth: Economic Theory and Political Discourse: Working Paper No 92', Grantham Research Institute on Climate Change and the Environment, London, 2012; A. Bowen and S. Fankhauser, 'The Green Growth Narrative: Paradigm Shift or Just Spin?' *Global Environmental Change*, 21, 4 (2011), pp.1157–59; OECD, '*OECD Environmental Outlook to 2050: The Consequences of Inaction*, Paris, 2012.

38 R. Heinberg, *Beyond the Limits to Growth*, Post Carbon Institute, Santa Rosa, CA, 2010; J. Martínez-Alier, U. Pascual, F. D. Vivien and E. Zaccai, 'Sustainable De-growth: Mapping the Context, Criticisms and Future Prospects of an Emergent Paradigm', *Ecological Economics*, 69, 9 (2010), pp.1741–47.

39 MED, 'New Zealand's Energy Outlook 2011: Reference Scenario and Sensitivity Analysis', Wellington, 2011.

40 MED, 'Greening New Zealand's Growth', Green Growth Advisory Group, Wellington, 2011.

41 F. Harvey, 'Cameron Set to Defend Coalition's Position on Green Economic Growth', *The Guardian*, 6 November 2012, www.theguardian.com/environment/2012/nov/05/cameron-poised-defend-green-economy (accessed 5 July 2015).

42 Pure Advantage, 'New Zealand's Position in the Green Race'; R. Boven, C. Harland and L. Grace, 'Navigating an Uncertain Future: Environmental Foundations for Long-term Success', Stakeholder Strategies, Auckland, 2012.

43 Royal Society of New Zealand, 'Facing the Future: Towards a Green Economy for New Zealand', Wellington, 2014; J. Renwick, R. Chapman et al., *Setting New Zealand's post-2020 Climate Target*, Royal Society of New Zealand, Wellington, 2015, www.royalsociety.org.nz/media/2015/06/Comments-on-setting-New-Zealands-post-2020-climate-change-

target.pdf (accessed 13 July 2015).

Chapter 5

1 H. W. J. Rittel and M. M. Webber, 'Dilemmas in a General Theory of Planning', *Policy Sciences*, 4, 2 (1973), pp.155–69; R. J. Lazarus, 'Super Wicked Problems and Climate Change: Restraining the Present to Liberate the Future', *Cornell Law Review*, 94 (2009), p.1153.

2 S. B. Pralle, 'Agenda-setting and Climate Change', *Environmental Politics*, 18, 5 (2009), pp.781–99; J. Boston, 'Evidence of Denial: The Case of Climate Change', *Stimulus: New Zealand Journal of Christian Thought and Practice*, 8, 3 (2010); K. Levin, B. Cashore, S. Bernstein and G. Auld, 'Overcoming the Tragedy of Super Wicked Problems: Constraining our Future Selves to Ameliorate Global Climate Change', *Policy Sciences*, 45, 2 (2012), pp.123–52.

3 A. Leiserowitz, E. Maibach, C. Roser-Renouf and J. Hmielowski, 'Global Warming's Six Americas in March 2012 and November 2011', Yale University and George Mason University, New Haven, CT, 2012.

4 S. C. Moser, 'Communicating Climate Change: History, Challenges, Process and Future Directions', *Wiley Interdisciplinary Reviews: Climate Change*, 1, 1 (2010), pp.31–53.

5 IEA, 'CO_2 Emissions from Fuel Combustion', *IEA Statistics*, Paris, 2011.

6 T. Steinfeldt, 'Cancun Conferees See Poor Public Understanding as Key Obstacle to Strong Action on Climate Change', Pew Centre on Global Climate Change, Washington DC, 2010.

7 J. Leslie, 'Is Canada Tarring Itself?', *New York Times*, 30 March 2014, www.nytimes.com/2014/03/31/opinion/is-canada-tarring-itself.html?_r= (accessed 5 July 2015).

8 A. White, 'We Need to Call Out Abbott's Climate Nihilism', *The Guardian*, 22 August 2014, www.theguardian.com/environment/southern-crossroads/2014/aug/22/tony-abbott-climate-denial-weathervane-nihilism (accessed 5 July 2015).

9 M. Kenny, 'Fairfax Ipsos Poll Shows Climate Change Concerns Heating up Around Tony Abbott', n = 1,401, *Sydney Morning Herald*, 9

December 2014, www.smh. com.au/federal-politics/ political-news/fairfax-ipsos-poll-shows-climate-change-concerns-heating-up-around-tony-abbott-20141208-122eus. html (accessed 5 July 2015).

10   B. Helm, 'Climate Change's Bottom Line', *New York Times*, 31 January 2015, www.nytimes. com/2015/02/01/business/ energy-environment/climate-changes-bottom-line.html (accessed 5 July 2015).

11   B. Gardiner, 'Setbacks Aside, Climate Change Is Finding Its Way Into the World's Classrooms', *New York Times*, 20 April 2014, www.nytimes. com/2014/04/21/business/ energy-environment/setbacks-aside-climate-change-is-finding-its-way-into-the-worlds-classrooms.html (accessed 5 July 2015).

12   J. Urry, *Climate Change and Society*, Polity Press, Cambridge, 2011.

13   S. Dietz and N. Stern, 'Endogenous Growth, Convexity of Damages and Climate Risk: How Nordhaus' Framework Supports Deep Cuts in Carbon Emissions', Working Paper No. 180, Centre for Climate Change Economics and Policy, London, 2014; M. L. Weitzman, 'Fat-tailed Uncertainty in the Economics of Catastrophic Climate Change', *Review of Environmental Economics and Policy*, 5, 2 (2011), pp.275–92.

14   G. M. Heal and A. Millner, 'Agreeing to Disagree on Climate Policy', *Proceedings of the National Academy of Sciences*, 111, 10 (2014); M. Schönfeld, 'Plan B: Global Ethics on Climate Change', *Journal of Global Ethics*, 7, 2 (2011), pp.129–36.

15   J. A. Nelson, 'Ethics and the Economist: What Climate Change Demands of Us', *Global Development and Environment Institute Working Papers*, Tufts University, Medford, MA, 2011.

16   George Monbiot, 'This Is About Us', www.monbiot. com/2009/12/14/this-is-about-us (accessed 5 July 2015).

17   Nicky Hager, 'Investigative Journalism in the Age of Media Meltdown: From National Party Headquarters to Afghanistan', www. brucejesson.com/?p=394 (accessed 5 July 2015).

18   D. Roberts, '"Brutal logic" and climate communications', grist.org/climate-change/2011-12-16-brutal-logic-and-climate-communications (accessed 5 July 2015).

19 J. Grantham, 'Be Persuasive. Be Brave. Be Arrested (if necessary)', *Nature*, 491, 303 (2012).

20 P. Barrett, 'Will Unchecked Global Warming Destroy Civilization by Century's End? What Three Degrees of Global Warming Really Means', *Policy Quarterly*, 2, 1 (2006), pp.5–9.

21 S. M. Hsiang, K. C. Meng and M. A. Cane, 'Civil Conflicts are Associated with the Global Climate', *Nature*, 476, 7361 (2011), pp.438–41.

22 US Joint Forces Command, 'The Joint Operating Environment 2010', Suffolk, VA, 2010.

23 A. Gurría, 'Climate: What's Changed, What Hasn't and What We Can Do About It – Six Months to COP21', lecture by Angel Gurría, Secretary-General, OECD, 3 July 2015, London, www.oecd.org/about/secretary-general/climate-what-has-changed-what-has-not-and-what-we-can-do-about-it.htm (accessed 13 July 2015).

24 A. Revkin, 'Climate Expert Says NASA Tried to Silence Him', *New York Times*, 29 January 2006, www.nytimes.com/2006/01/29/science/earth/29climate.

html?pagewanted=all (accessed 5 July 2015).

25 A. J. Hoffman, 'Talking Past Each Other? Cultural Framing of Skeptical and Convinced Logics in the Climate Change Debate', *Organization & Environment*, 24, 1 (2011), pp.3–33.

26 N. Mabey, J. Gulledge, B. Finel and K. Silverthorne, 'Degrees of Risk: Defining a Risk Management Framework for Climate Security', E3G, London, 2011.

27 K. Anderson, 'Climate Change Going Beyond Dangerous – Brutal Numbers and Tenuous Hope', *Development Dialogue*, (September 2012).

28 New Zealand Climate Change Research Institute, K. Trenberth, 'The Russian Heat Wave and Other Recent Climate Extremes', Wellington, 2011.

29 N. Oreskes and E. M. Conway, 'The Collapse of Western Civilization: A View from the Future', *Daedalus*, 142, 1 (2013), pp.40–58.

30 C. Hamilton, 'What History Can Teach Us About Climate Change Denial', in S. Weintrobe (ed.), *Engaging with Climate Change: Psychoanalytic and*

Interdisciplinary Perspectives, Routledge, London, 2012.

31 L. Hymas, 'Energy and Environment in the GOP Platform: They Said What?', grist.org/politics/energy-and-environment-in-the-gop-platform-they-said-what (accessed 5 July 2015).

32 World Economic Forum, 'Global Risks 2015 (10th Edition)', Geneva, 2015.

Chapter 6

1 R. Wright, *A Short History of Progress*, Carroll & Graf Publishers, New York, 2005.

2 A. Schendler and M. Trexler, 'The Coming Climate Panic?', grist.org/article/2009-12-23-the-coming-climate-panic (accessed 5 July 2015).

3 G. Monbiot, 'Climate Change? Try Catastrophic Climate Breakdown', *The Guardian*, 27 September 2013, www.theguardian.com/environment/georgemonbiot/2013/sep/27/ipcc-climate-change-report-global-warming (accessed 13 July 2015).

4 G. Marshall, 'Why Our Brains are Wired to Ignore Climate Change and What To Do About It', *The Guardian*, 23 September 2014, www.theguardian.com/commentisfree/2014/sep/23/why-our-brains-wired-ignore-climate-change-united-nations (accessed 13 July 2015).

ACKNOWLEDGEMENTS

My thanks to Peter Barrett, James Renwick, Catherine Leining, Philippa Howden-Chapman, Amy Howden-Chapman, Harry Chapman and Sarah Burgess for valuable comments. The author is responsible for any remaining errors.

ABOUT THE AUTHOR

Dr Ralph Chapman is Associate Professor and Director of the Graduate Programme in Environmental Studies at Victoria University of Wellington. He is a frequent writer and speaker on the policy implications of climate change for New Zealand, particularly in the areas of energy, transport, housing and urban policies. His experience includes working in the Treasury (New Zealand and the UK), the Ministry for the Environment, the Beehive, and with the OECD. He was a negotiator of the Kyoto Protocol for the New Zealand government. Dr Chapman is a member of the research team that was presented with the 2014 Prime Minister's Science Prize.

ABOUT BWB TEXTS

BWB Texts are short books on big subjects: succinct narratives spanning history, memoir, contemporary issues, science and more from great New Zealand writers. All BWB Texts are available digitally, with selected works also in paperback. New Texts are published monthly – visit www.bwb.co.nz to see the latest releases.

BWB Texts include:

Paul Callaghan: Luminous Moments
Foreword by Catherine Callaghan

Creeks and Kitchens: A Childhood Memoir
Maurice Gee

The Quiet War on Asylum
Tracey Barnett

Thorndon: Wellington and Home: My Katherine Mansfield Project
Kirsty Gunn

The Inequality Debate: An Introduction
Max Rashbrooke

Wellbeing Economics: Future Directions for New Zealand
Paul Dalziel & Caroline Saunders

Growing Apart: Regional Prosperity in New Zealand
Shamubeel Eaqub

Barefoot Years
Martin Edmond

The Piketty Phenomenon: New Zealand Perspectives
Various

The Child Poverty Debate: Myths, Misconceptions and Misunderstandings
Jonathan Boston & Simon Chapple

Ruth, Roger and Me: Debts and Legacies
Andrew Dean

On Coming Home
Paula Morris

Haerenga: Early Māori Journeys Across the Globe
Vincent O'Malley

Generation Rent: Rethinking New Zealand's Priorities
Shamubeel & Selena Eaqub